u and Jane Short

IELTS Graduation

Study Skills

MACMILLAN

Macmillan Education
Between Towns Road, Oxford OX4 3PP
A division of Macmillan Publishers Limited
Companies and representatives throughout the world

ISBN: 978-1-4050-8076-7

Designed by eMC Design; www.emcdesign.org.uk
Illustrated by Peter Cornwell and Peters & Zabransky.
Cover design by Andrew Oliver
Cover photograph supplied by Alamy.

Authors' acknowledgements
Jane Short would like to thank her children, Leon and Laura, for their patience and support during the
writing of the book. Charlie Martineau would like to thank Rob, Janet, Mollie and all his colleagues
at Harrogate Language Academy. Thank you to Amanda Anderson and everyone at Macmillan for
managing the process.

The publishers would like to thank Mary Jane Hogan for commenting on the material.

The authors and publishers would like to thank the following for permission to use copyright material:
Extract from 'Cruel to be kind' by Vanessa Woods Cosmos magazine, no. 8 reprinted by permission
of the author; Extract from 'Focus on Interests' by Steven P Cohen from Entrepreneurial Edge, Vol 4,
1998, copyright © Steven P Cohen, The Negotiation Skills Company Inc. www.negotiationskills.com ;
Extract from 'International travel: record number of visits to UK in 2004' National Statistics website:
www.statistics.co.uk Crown copyright material is reproduced with the permission of the Controller
of HMSO; Extract from 'How hypnosis works' from web 'Howstuffworks' www.howstuffworks.com ;
Adapted extract from 'More media, less news' published in The Economist 24/8/06, copyright © The
Economist Newspaper Limited, London, 2006, reprinted by permission of the publisher; Adapted
extract from 'When the door is always open' published in The Economist 24/10/02, copyright © The
Economist Newspaper Limited, London, 2002, reprinted by permission of the publisher; Extract from
'Why computer games are good for your child' by Jimmy Leach, copyright © Guardian Newspaper
Limited 2006, first published in Guardian Unlimited 17/3/06, reprinted by permission of the publisher;
Extract from 'Sea levels likely to rise much faster than was predicted' by Steve Connor, copyright © The
Independent 2006, first published in The Independent 17/2/06, reprinted by permission of the publisher;
Extract from 'Vegetarianism: the choice of the more intelligent child' by Jeremy Laurance copyright ©
The Independent 2006, first published in The Independent 15/12/06, reprinted by permission of the
publisher; Extract from 'A funding call for nutrition' website 2/3/06, copyright © The International Bank
for Reconstruction and Development/The World Bank; Extract from 'The beginning of architecture' from
Why buildings stand up: The Strength of Architecture by Mario Salvadori, copyright © 1980 by Mario
Salvadori used by permission of W. W. Norton & Company, Inc.; Extract from 'Wives are outnumbered
by single and divorced women for the first time' by Sarah Womack copyright © Telegraph Group Limited
2006, first published in The Daily Telegraph 19/12/06, reprinted by permission of the publisher; Extract
from Macmillan English Dictionary For Advanced Learners (Macmillan Publishers Limited, 2002), text ©
Bloomsbury Publishing Plc 2002, reprinted by permission of the publisher.

The authors and publishers would like to thank the following for permission to reproduce their
photographic material: BananaStock p84; Brand X Pictures pp19, 20, 35, 43; Image100 p79; Photodisc
p29, 77; Pixtal p8; Rubberball Productions p27.
Pie chart p41 and graph p46 reproduced with the kind permission of The Economist © The Economist
Newspaper Limited, London (Oct 24th 2002).
Graphs pp 35, 49(fig.2, fig.4, fig.6), 57, 59, 61(all), 107 reproduced with the kind permission of United
Kingdom National Statistics.

Printed in Thailand

2012 2011 2010
11 10 9 8 7 6 5

Contents

Introduction

Welcome to *IELTS Graduation Study Skills*. This book provides you with exam practice materials and will also:

- Encourage you to develop useful examination skills that will help you increase your IELTS score.
- Teach you about the various question types you will encounter in IELTS and the most effective ways to answer them.

Each section of this book corresponds to one of the four IELTS modules. You are encouraged to develop your skills by doing focused exercises. Detailed guidance is given in the key. In the skills practice sections, you are given the opportunity to practise what you have learned. At the end of the book there is a complete Practice test.

As IELTS Graduation is aimed at students starting at around 5.5, the reading and listening texts are similar in length and difficulty to those in IELTS.

Model answers and sample student answers are given for both Writing and Speaking sections. Useful language is provided. This enables you to evaluate your own work.

This book is appropriate for self study, but could also be used as the basis for a short intensive IELTS preparation course.

The IELTS Exam

IELTS, or the International English Language Testing System, is an exam designed to assess your level of English, on a scale from 1-9. The score you need will depend upon the course and the university you want to study at, but many students find they need to get an overall band score of 6.

Each section is weighted equally, but it is possible to get half band scores for the Reading and Listening modules (eg 5.5, or 6.5), but only whole number bands (eg 5, 6, 7 etc) for Speaking and Writing. Overall, therefore, you may get a half band score.

Band 9 – Expert User
Has fully operational command of the language: appropriate, accurate and fluent with complete understanding.

Band 8 – Very Good User
Has fully operational command of the language with only occasional unsystematic inaccuracies and inappropriacies. Misunderstandings may occur in unfamiliar situations. Handles complex detailed argumentation well.

Band 7 – Good User
Has operational command of the language, though with occasional inaccuracies, inappropriacies and misunderstandings in some situations. Generally handles complex language well and understands detailed reasoning.

Band 6 – Competent User
Has generally effective command of the language despite some inaccuracies, inappropriacies and misunderstandings. Can use and understand fairly complex language, particularly in familiar situations.

Band 5 – Modest User
Has partial command of the language, coping with overall meaning in most situations, though is likely to make many mistakes. Should be able to handle basic communication in own field.

Band 4 – Limited User
Basic competence is limited to familiar situations. Has frequent problems in understanding and expression. Is not able to use complex language.

Band 3 – Extremely Limited User
Conveys and understands only general meaning in very familiar situations. Frequent breakdowns in communication can occur.

Band 2 – Intermittent User
No real communication is possible except for the most basic information using isolated words or short formulae in familiar situations and to meet immediate needs. Has great difficulty in understanding spoken and written English.

Band 1 – Non User
Essentially has no ability to use the language beyond possibly a few isolated words.

Band 0 – Did not attempt the test
No assessable information provided.

A summary of each module is outlined below:

Listening

The Listening takes about 40 minutes and each section gets progressively more difficult.

Part	Number of speakers	Number of questions	Situation	Example
1	2	10	social/general	Conversation between a student and a tutor
2	1	10	social/general	Introductory talk for a group of new students
3	2–4	10	academic	Students discussing project work
4	1	10	academic	A lecture given to an academic audience

Question Types: multiple choice, completing notes or sentences, completing or labelling diagrams, charts or tables, classifying, matching and writing short answers.

Exam Tips: Each section is only heard ONCE. Time is given to look quickly at the questions before each part is played. You should write your answers on the question paper during the exam and, at the end, you are given 10 minutes to transfer your answers to your answer sheet. Mistakes will cost you marks, so be careful when transferring your answers and check grammar and spelling.

Academic Reading.

The Reading lasts one hour and there are three reading texts, of increasing difficulty, taken from newspapers, magazines, books and journals. The topics are of general interest, so learners do not have to be experts in the subject area to understand them.

Question Types: multiple choice, choosing *true/ false/ not given*, or *yes/ no/ not given*, identifying the view of the writer, completing sentences or notes, completing or labelling diagrams, charts or tables, classifying, matching, choosing paragraph headings and writing short answers. There are 40 questions in total.

Exam Tips: You need to write your answers on an answer sheet. You are not given extra time to do this, so you must learn how to manage your time (20 minutes for each section), so that you can finish the whole module within the hour. You can do this by reading quickly and efficiently.

Academic Writing

There are two tasks in this module and it lasts 1 hour.

Task	Time	Number of-words	Description of task
1	20 minutes	At least 150 words	Describe, compare and contrast information in diagrams, charts or tables, *or* describe the stages of a process, *or* explain how something works
2	40 minutes	At least 250 words	Give solutions to a problem, *or* present arguments in favour and against an opinion, *or* give and justify an opinion.

Assessment: In order to do well in Task 1, it is important to answer the question clearly, and organize your answer well. This may include grouping data appropriately and describing trends, rather than detailing every piece of information given. Your answer also needs to be accurate and include a good range of vocabulary.

In Task 2 slightly different assessment criteria are used. Here you need to ensure that you answer the question and include a clear and logical argument, giving evidence or examples where appropriate. Your answer also needs to be well organized and have a variety of vocabulary and grammatical structures used accurately.

Exam Tips: Timing is very important. Task 2 is longer and you can score more marks that Task 1. Word limits are important. Writing less than the number of words stated will result in a lower score.

Speaking

The Speaking module takes between 11 and 14 minutes and is an oral interview between the learner and an examiner. It will be recorded on audio tape.

Part	Time	Description
1	4–5 minutes	General questions about home, family, studies, etc.
2	3–4 minutes	You are given a card with a topic and 3–4 prompt questions on it. You have 1 minute to prepare, and then have to speak for 1–2 minutes on that topic. At the end, the examiner may ask you a question.
3	4–5 minutes	Further discussion questions relating to the subject in part 2. This section requires you to give opinions, speculate and express reasons.

Assessment: Assessment is based on your fluency, the range, and accuracy of the vocabulary and grammatical structures you use, and your pronunciation.

Exam Tips: You need to give longer answers to questions, rather than simple 'Yes' or 'No' replies. It is important to practise speaking for 1–2 minutes on various topics. Memorizing long speeches is not a good idea; examiners will ask you to talk about another subject. Relax as much as possible during the exam.

Study Skills: Listening

How much do you know about the IELTS Listening module?
Read the information in the box, then do the quiz below to find out.

Information on listening test

In the IELTS listening test there are 40 questions, divided into four sections of ten questions each. The listening test lasts 30 minutes, but you will have some time to read the questions before you listen and 30 seconds to check your answers at the end of each section.

In Section 1 you will hear a dialogue on a social topic and in Section 2 you will hear one speaker giving information in a social situation. The listening texts in Sections 3 and 4 take place in an academic context and consist of a discussion between two to four speakers for Section 3 and a talk or lecture given by one speaker for Section 4.

Quiz

1   In which section (**1–4**) of the listening test might you hear the following situations?
   ❏ **A** A professor gives a lecture about the history of the UK school system.
   ❏ **B** A man asks for information about renting a car.
   ❏ **C** Two students discuss their university coursework.
   ❏ **D** A manager gives a talk about the facilities at the sports centre.

2   Which of the following are question types in the IELTS listening test?
   A Multiple choice
   B Classifying information

   C Grammar transformation
   D Short-answer questions
   E Labelling a map or diagram
   F Completing a table
   G Completing a summary
   H Drawing a diagram
   I Matching information with descriptions or opinions
   J Completing a sentence

3   Which accents will you hear in the IELTS listening test?

4   How many times will you hear the recording?

Section 1

Listening section 1: Exam information
Number of speakers: two (a dialogue)
Context: a conversation on a social topic
Example situation: a student applying for a parking permit or someone reporting a stolen bag

Note, table, form, summary and diagram completion tasks

Skills development

Remember
- If you are asked to fill in a form, complete a table, a flow chart or some notes, you are *not* expected to write full sentences.
- In summary completion tasks you will be asked to use the *exact* words from the listening text to complete a grammatically correct summary.

Tip
Just after you hear the words 'Now turn to Section 1', you will hear a description of the context, or situation, of the listening text.
For example: 'Mary is calling a travel agent to find the cheapest way to get to Australia' or 'You will hear a telephone conversation between a new student and the accommodation officer.'
By listening carefully to this brief introduction, you should be able to predict the number of speakers, the topic of conversation and some of the vocabulary you can expect to hear.

Prediction

1 🎧 **01** Listen to the introduction to Section 1 and answer the following questions.

1 How many speakers are you going to hear?
2 What is the topic of the conversation?

2 Look at the journey details below. What kind of information will you be listening for in questions **1–5**? Write the kind of information in the gaps below.

Question 1   ....
Question 2   a number, day, week or month
Question 3   ....
Question 4   ....
Question 5   ....

Check your answers on page 98.

> **Remember**
> Identify the kind of information you are listening for. This may be, for example, a number, a name, a date, a time, a length of time, or a detailed piece of information.

Completing notes

🎧 **02** Listen and complete the notes. Write **NO MORE THAN THREE WORDS AND/OR A NUMBER** for each answer.

> **Journey details**
> Destination/town: **(1)** _Harrogate_
> Time/date of travel: **(2)** _Next week tues thursday._
> Possible means of transport: bus or train
> Train: change in York or **(3)** _Leeds_
> Bus: stops **(4)** _3_ times en route
> Bus or train: a couple of hours slower **(5)** _by bus coach_

Skills development

In this exercise you are going to practise predicting the content of questions **6–12**.

1 Look at questions **6–12** on page 9. What kind of information will you be listening for in these questions?

Question 6   ....
Question 7   ....
Question 8   a type of ticket
Question 9   ....
Question 10   ....
Question 11   ....
Question 12   ....

Check your answers on page 98.

> **Tip**
> Use grammatical clues to select possible answers.

Study Skills: Listening

2 Look at questions **6–12** below again and <u>underline</u> the possible answers to each question.

Question 6 **A** train **B** month **C** Monday **D** journey **E** week
Question 7 **A** midday **B** morning **C** 5.30 **D** early evening **E** first thing
Question 8 **A** cheap **B** return **C** single **D** credit card **E** reservation
Questions 9 and 12 **A** 2 o'clock **B** in the morning **C** a long time **D** 3 hours
                                E a discount
Questions 10 and 11 **A** 5 pm **B** ten o'clock **C** 6 hours **D** the afternoon
                                E a different time on Wednesday

Check your answers on page 98.

Completing a sentence

03 Listen and complete the sentences in questions **6–12**. Write (NO MORE THAN THREE WORDS AND/OR A NUMBER) for each answer.

The customer wants to travel on (6) ....Thursday........ at approximately (7) ....@ 2: p.m.... . The customer wants to buy a (8) ....one way.... ticket. The train from London to Harrogate takes (9) ....2: 31 p.... and leaves at (10) ....4:30.... The coach leaves at (11) ....2: p.m.... and takes (12) ....2:45 min....

Check your answers on page 98.

Skills development

Completing a table

1 Look at tables 1 and 2 and predict the topic of each dialogue. Check your answers on page 98.

2 Circle the kind of information you would need to complete tables 1 and 2. Check your answers on page 98.

numbers	days of the week	times of day
names	months	length of time
letters	years	%

Table 1

	Busy Clouds Airline
1 fare	
2 discount fare	
3 arriving/departing	
4 booking code	

numbers	days of the week	times of day
names	months	length of time
letters	years	%

Table 2

	Etherway Satellite Services
1 minimum term	
2 monthly payment	
3 channels	
4 installation fee	

3 04 Listen and complete the table for questions **13–16** below. Write **NO MORE THAN THREE WORDS AND/OR A NUMBER** for each answer.

information

headings →

	Train	Bus
name of discount card	(13) ...Railcard...	student discount card
% discount	(14) ...25%...	20%
standard fare	£16.50	(15) ...20...
cost of discount card	£20	(16) ...15...

Remember
Even if your answer is right in the listening test, you will lose marks for incorrect spelling. It is very important to learn how to spell common names, like capital cities and countries, days of the week, months, and words that sound similar but have different spellings, for example, *practice* (noun) and *practise* (verb).

Skills development

Listening for letters and numbers

By practising your own pronunciation you can improve your listening skills. This exercise will help you recognize and pronounce letters of the alphabet.

1 05 How do you pronounce these letters? Read them out loud to yourself and then listen and compare your pronunciation with that of the speaker on the recording. Circle the letters that sound different. Practise them by repeating them to a friend or recording them and comparing them with the original until they sound similar.

```
B C D E G P T V
A H J K
F L M N S X Z
I Y
O
R
Q U W
```

Information
If you are told to write **NO MORE THAN TWO WORDS AND/OR A NUMBER**, then 3.14, for example, counts as one number. The phone number 529783 is one number, not six.

In this exercise you will practise saying numbers to help you recognize them more easily in a listening text.

2 06 Read the following numbers and symbols out loud to yourself, and then listen to them on the recording. If you can record your pronunciation, it will be easier to compare it with that of the speaker on the recording. Read the numbers again until they sound similar.

1 0870 225225
2 6.5
3 6.75
4 6½
5 9.20pm
6 9.45am
7 / (as in: www.macmillan.com/academic)
8 @ (as in: audiobooks@macmillan.co.uk)
9 • (as in: www.macmillan.com)

3 07 Listen and write down the numbers, times, dates and quantities you hear.

1 .....1998...............
2 .....Aug. 13th...........
3 .....£40.40p............
4 .....2½ hour............
5 .....97 miles............
6 .....1 to...............
7 .....5 hours.............
8 .....2.00p..............

4 08 Listen and complete the sentences.

1 There's a train leaving London .....Euston..... at two thirty.
2 There's one at two o'clock from .....Victoria..... Coach Station.
3 The postcode is .....HG2 1JL.....
4 The surname is .....FAUVELL.....
5 I've got an offer from .....Birmingham..... University.
6 124 .....WAWACK..... Road.
7 The postcode is .....PB7 9RL.....
8 It arrives in .....Manchester..... at 16.41.

Check your answers on page 98.

Completing notes and tables

Questions 1–4

09 Listen to the conversation and complete the notes below. Write **NO MORE THAN THREE WORDS AND/OR A NUMBER** for each answer.

Remember
Read the notes carefully before you listen and decide what kind of information you will be listening for.

Dentist

Location: near(1) .....Harbour.....

Name: Mr J. (2) .....Dount.....

Telephone: (3) .....4296261.....

Address: 59 (4) .....Raddlebath..... Road

Questions 5–10

🔊 **10** Listen to the conversation and complete the table below. Write **NO MORE THAN THREE WORDS AND/OR A NUMBER** for each answer.

	Emergency appointment	Monthly insurance	Regular check-up
Normal price	(5) ...~~£60~~...	(8) ...~~£15~~...	—
Student discount	(6) ...~~£ 20/~~...	—	(10) ...~~£45~~...
Student price	(7) ...~~£48~~...	(9) ...~~~~...	—

Section 2

> **Remember**
> For multiple-choice questions, look at the question *stem* to identify the topic of the question (eg university accommodation) and the *options* to find out what aspects of the topic (eg types of accommodation, cost, advantages/ disadvantages) you need to focus on while you are listening.

> **Listening section 2: Exam information**
> Number of speakers: one (a monologue)
> Context: non-academic; a social situation
> Example situation: an informal talk on how to open a bank account

Multiple-choice questions

> **Information**
> There are two common types of multiple-choice question in the IELTS listening test. In the first type, you will be given the first part of a sentence and will have to complete it from several options. In the second type, you will be asked a question and will have to select the answer from a list of options.

Skills development

Prediction

Before you listen, look at multiple-choice questions **1–4** below and answer the following questions about what you may hear on the recording.

1 Where is the talk taking place?
2 Who could be speaking?
3 Who is the talk intended for?

Check your answers on page 99.

4 <u>Underline</u> the key words in the question stems to identify the main topics of the talk.
5 Look at the options in each question and decide what kind of information you will be listening for.

Check your answers on page 99.

Key words and synonyms

> **Remember**
> The words on the IELTS Listening question paper may be different from those in the listening text. Find the key words in the questions and think of alternative words with the same meaning (synonyms).

Look at the following key words from questions **1–4** and use a thesaurus to find synonyms.

1 situated   ....
2 all over   ....
3 individual   ....
4 managed   ....
5 widest   ....
6 collection   ....

Check your answers on page 99.

Study Skills: Listening

11 Listen to the talk and answer questions **1–4**. Circle the appropriate letter.

1 The university is situated
   A on a campus.
   B in different buildings all over town.
   C outside the town.

2 The individual colleges work
   A separately from the university.
   B together to form the university.
   C independently of each other.

3 Examinations are managed by
   A the Colleges.
   B the Director of Studies.
   C the Faculties.

4 The library with the widest collection of books is
   A the College library.
   B the Faculty library.
   C the University Library.

Check your answers on page 99.

Skills development

> **Information**
> In some multiple-choice questions in the IELTS test, you will be asked to answer a question by selecting **MORE THAN ONE OPTION** from a list. You can approach these questions systematically.

► **Strategy**

   i   Circle the **NUMBER OF OPTIONS** you are asked to select on the question paper.
   ii Underline the key words in the stem.
   iii While you are listening, tick the options that are mentioned in the recording.
   iv Some of the options may be mentioned, but may *not* be the correct answer. Listen carefully for words that indicate that an option is *not* correct, eg *not*, *unlike*, *but*, *isn't*, *aren't*.

11 Now follow steps **i–iv** for question **5**. Listen and circle **TWO** appropriate letters.

5 Which **TWO** of the following services are provided by the Colleges?
   A Sports facilities
   B Academic direction
   C Counselling services
   D Accommodation
   E Health advice

Check your answer on page 99.

Remember
Each listening text in Sections 1, 2 and 3 is divided into two or three parts to test different listening skills. There is always a short time between them to study the questions.

Types of map questions: Revising locations and labelling a map

Look at the floor plan and match the rooms with the locations in the list below.

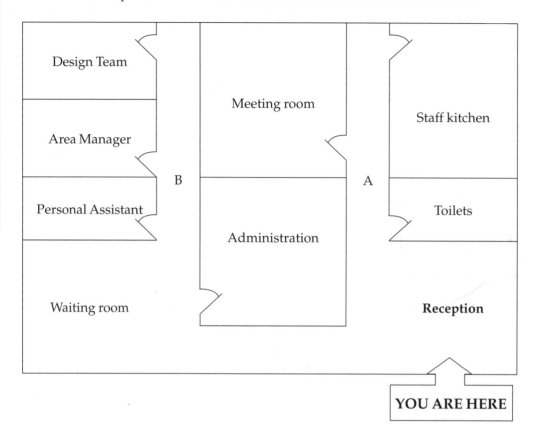

Area Manager	between reception and the staff kitchen
Administration	opposite the staff kitchen
Personal Assistant	in corridor B, second door on the left
Staff kitchen	in corridor B, opposite Administration
Toilets	in corridor B, first door on the right
Meeting room	at the end of corridor B, on the left
Design Team	in corridor A, last door on the right

Questions 6–10

12 Listen to the speaker describing the facilities in the town. Complete the labels on the map. Write **NO MORE THAN TWO WORDS** for each answer.

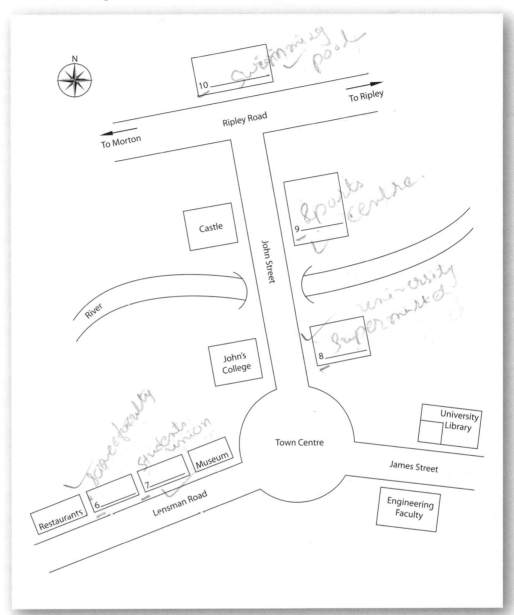

Skills development

Completing summaries

Although you only have a short time to read the question before you listen, you can prepare by following the steps below:

i   Scan the incomplete summary and <u>underline</u>/(circle) the *key words*. These will usually be words or phrases that are repeated in the text.

ii Identify the *topic* by classifying the key words (eg mountain, sea, riverbanks = geography/ecology).

iii Look for numbers and dates, or words beginning with capital letters, indicating names and places, to help you identify the *context* of the listening text (time, place and people speaking).

iv Identify *grammatical possibilities* by looking at the words on either side of the gaps.

Look at this summary and follow the steps above.

The union is the centre of student (1) _Social life_ It has two
(2) _bathe_ and a (3) _two live bands_ at weekends. There
are also (4) _Sports_ clubs and (5) _supportive Activity_ that
encourage leisure activities.
The union's formal functions are to (6) .... student interests.
The executive is responsible for (7 _good Relation_ that affect students. In
addition, they advance student (8) .... at university board
meetings. The union executive works with (9) .... to foster
positive relations between the university and the town. The local union collaborates
with other (10) ....

Check your answers on page 99.

13 Listen to the speaker describing the functions of the Student Union.
Complete the summary above. Write **NO MORE THAN TWO WORDS** for each
answer.

Check your answers on page 100.

Section 3

> **Listening section 3: Exam information**
> Number of speakers: between two and four
> Context: academic
> Example situations: a tutor and a student discussing an assignment; a seminar with a few
> students talking together

Identifying the speakers

This is easy when there is only one woman or one man in the conversation. When
there are two men, two women, or perhaps three speakers, you need to identify the
speakers at the beginning of the conversation.

Skills development

Synonyms and paraphrasing

On page 12, you practised finding synonyms for key words in the question stems. In
the exercise below, practise re-phrasing statements without changing their meaning.
This will prepare you to listen for alternative expressions in the listening text.

Look at these students' opinions of several of their lecturers. Write alternative
sentences to express the same ideas.

1   Miss Davies is well worth listening to.

....

2. Dr Preston? Not a great speaker but a real expert on climatology.

....

3. Never dull, always useful.

....

4. McEnroe has really good days, but he has bad ones too!

....

Check your answers on page 100.

Classifying questions

Read sentences **1–4** and decide whether they mean **A**, **B** or **C**. You may have to use
the same option more than once.

A Always relevant
B Good sometimes
C Good on certain subjects

> **Remember**
> The language in Section
> 3 is more complex than
> in Sections 1 and 2. The
> discussion contains a large
> amount of information and
> you will be asked to listen
> for specific details. You will
> be expected to identify the
> speakers' attitudes and
> opinions. The vocabulary
> in Section 3 is also more
> complex. Listen carefully
> for synonyms and parallel
> expressions.

> **Remember**
> • The introduction to the
>   listening will usually tell
>   you something about the
>   speakers.
> • Speakers will use each
>   other's names, at least
>   at the beginning of the
>   recording.
> • Speakers often have
>   different accents, which
>   can help you keep the
>   identities clear in your
>   mind.

1 Miss Davies is well worth listening to.
2 Dr Preston? Not a great speaker but a real expert on climatology.
3 Never dull, always useful.
4 McEnroe has really good days, but he has bad ones too.

Check your answers on page 100.

Skills practice

Dialogue 1

Questions 1–5

14 Listen to the conversation and complete the sentences below. Write **NO MORE THAN THREE WORDS** for each answer.

Angela's study strategy

1 She ..... _Planned_ ..... her work for the year thoroughly.
2 She ..... _prep'd_ ..... of all the work she needed to do before the final exams. _Prepare list (a)_
3 In this way she was able to make ..... _timetable_ ..... and follow it.
4 This was helpful because she covered all the necessary topics and was ..... about how much she could do.
5 At the beginning of the year she chose her ..... _Subject_ ..... carefully to avoid being overloaded with work.

Questions 6–10

15 What does Angela suggest to Steve about the following authors? Choose your answers from the box and write the letters **A–C** next to questions **6–10**.

A Don't read	
B Read conclusion	
C Must read	
6 Bradley:	C
7 Holland:	C
8 Johnson:	C
9 Murry:	A
10 Richards:	B

Dialogue 2

Questions 1–6

16 What aspects of their project do Jim and Kimberly decide to include in their presentation? Choose your answers from the box and write the letters **A–C** next to questions **1–6**.

A Must include	
B Only if there's time	
C Don't discuss	
1 An overview	A
2 Products	A
3 Accounts	A b C
4 Marketing	A
5 Roleplay	B
6 Questions	C B

Short answer questions

Remember

In this type of question you may be asked to answer a question in two or three words and/or a number, or to make a list of items from the listening text. You are not expected to write complete sentences and you must *not* write more than the number of words indicated on the question sheet.

Questions 7–12

🔊 **17** Answer the questions below. Write **NO MORE THAN THREE WORDS** for each answer.

Name **TWO** things Jim and Kimberly enjoyed about the project.

7 ~~X~~ *Business* ....

8 ✓ *profit* ....

What **TWO** aspects of the project surprised Jim and Kimberly?

9 *hardwork* ....

10 *time consuming* ....

List **TWO** differences between the project and real life.

11 ~~X~~ *Accounts* ....

12 *Detailed the business plan* ....

Section 4

> **Listening section 4: Exam information**
> Number of speakers: one
> Context: academic
> Example situation: a lecture. The subject may be quite specific, but you do not need any specialist knowledge to answer the questions, as all the information you need is included in the listening text.

Skills development

Understanding the question: Skimming

Skimming is a rapid reading technique that will give you a general overview of the topic of a question. Use this technique to identify the key words or their synonyms in the questions and the options. Key words are usually repeated in both the question and the listening text.

Underline the key words in questions 1–5 to identify the *topic* of each question. Question 1 has been done for you.

Check your answers on page 100.

Remember

The listening text in Section 4 is longer than those in Sections 1–3. As you only have 40 seconds to read the questions, analyse them quickly. Identify the topic and the kind of information you need to answer the question. To identify the topic *skim* through the questions for key words. To find out what kind of information you need you should *scan* for question words and detail.

To review, refer to the prediction strategies in Section 1, pages 8–9.

Questions 1–5

1 Which (THREE reasons) are given for the development of construction site logistics management over the last twenty years?
   - **A** building operations more complex
   - **B** wider variety of specialists
   - **C** higher pay for experts
   - **D** more sophisticated machinery
   - **E** industry more responsible to community

2 Which **TWO** of the following services are **NOT** supplied by logistics management?
   - **A** labour
   - **B** quantity surveyors
   - **C** equipment and machinery
   - **D** administrative services
   - **E** accommodation

3 **THREE** big projects specifically mentioned in the lecture which are typically controlled by site logistics management are:

   A road building
   B tunnel-digging ✓
   C bridge-construction
   D building a power station ✓
   E building a department store ✓

4 **TWO** benefits of logistics management for the construction industry are:

   A improved cash flow
   B more time for specialization ✓
   C more security for staff
   D reduced expenditure ✓
   E permanent employment

5 Which **TWO** of the following career advantages do **NOT** apply to logistics management for individuals?

   A long-term contracts ✓
   B travel abroad
   C guaranteed employment
   D a variety of job prospects
   E flexible working conditions

Check your answers on page 100.

Understanding the question: Scanning

When you *scan* a text, you are looking for specific information or detail.

Scan questions **1–5** and **circle** the words that indicate the **kind of information** you are expected to listen for and the **number of options** you should choose. Question 1 has been done for you.

Check your answers on page 100.

Skills practice

In this section, you will practise answering multiple-choice questions in which you have to choose the correct **TWO** or **THREE** items from a list of five or more.

Questions 1–5

18 Listen to the lecture and answer questions **1–5** above.

Check your answers on page 100.

Skills development

Signpost language

Certain words and phrases are used in spoken language to guide the listener. In a lecture, signpost language would be used to indicate, for example: the structure of a lecture, a new topic, the next step in an argument or the next stage of a process, a comparison or a contrasting idea, a reference to a previous comment, or a conclusion.

The following expressions are taken from Recording script 19. Complete the table below with letters **A–O** and check your answers on page 100. **C** has been done for you as an example.

A	to begin with	**I**	so
B	although	**J**	as I've already implied
C	looking at	**K**	think about
D	so that	**L**	a decade ago
E	now let's turn to	**M**	and then
F	the first thing to say is	**N**	and secondly
G	for instance	**O**	today
H	but		

Function	Phrase
1 Introducing/focusing on a new topic	C ✓
2 Tracing a chronological process	A
3 Contrasting ideas	B ✓
4 Giving an example	G
5 Indicating steps in a logical argument	A/N
6 Indicating the structure of a lecture	L
7 Referring to a previous comment	J

Skills practice

Questions 1–6

19 Listen to Part 1 of the careers lecture on work in retailing. Choose words from the box to complete the summary.

designer outlets	online	customer
internet	graduates	non-specialists
verticals	business sector	
technology	experts	

Modern-day retailing is a dynamic (1) .... which reacts rapidly to fashion trends and technological advances. Nowadays, approaches to sales range from personal contact with the (2) .... in traditional stores, to online commerce (3) .... who want to enter retailing may study Business Management or Information Technology at university. But the retail industry encourages ambitious (4) .... with experience in the business. In recent times, the retail trade has changed dramatically, as a result of the growth of small specialized companies, known as (5) ...., which sell through the internet and from (6) ...., brand-name boutiques, catalogues and high street chains.

Remember
The questions follow the same order as the information in the listening text. Once you have answered a question, you will not be expected to refer to previous information again.

Questions 7–10

20 Listen to the talk about the use of technology in the retail sector and label the diagram below. Choose your answers from the box and write the correct letters next to questions **7–10** on the flow chart.

Remember
You will have 10 minutes to transfer your answers to the answer sheet at the end of the test. You must complete the answer sheet in pencil. Spend these 10 minutes:

- checking your spelling is correct
- making sure you put the right answer in the right box
- checking any answers you have left blank. Try to remember what you heard and make a guess. It is better to make a guess than to leave a blank.

A active	D hand-held	G on a pallet
B bar codes	E internet connection	H passive
C computer	F network	I part of a till

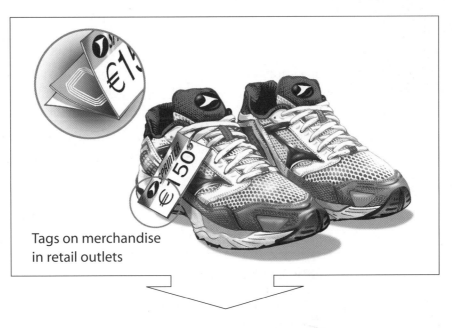

Tags on merchandise in retail outlets

are read by an apparatus which is

(7) ....Active A.......   **or**   (8) ....H..........

and which sends the information to a

(9) ....C ✓

which is linked to a

(10) ....E

Check your answers on page 100.

Study Skills: Reading

How much do you know about the IELTS Academic Reading module? Do the quiz below to find out.

Now check your answers on page 101.

Quiz

Answer True (T) or False (F).

1 It lasts 60 minutes. ❏

2 You get extra time to copy your answers onto your answer sheet. ❏

3 There are four texts. ❏

4 You should expect one text to contain detailed logical argument. ❏

5 There are about 12–14 questions with each text. ❏

6 The questions get progressively more difficult. ❏

7 Spelling is not important. ❏

8 You have to answer the passages in the order they appear on the question paper. ❏

9 You can write your answers in pen. ❏

10 You can predict the questions. ❏

11 Reading popular magazines and novels is good preparation. ❏

12 This book will help me get a much better score in a short time. ❏

Reading Passage 1

Skills development

Skimming

Skimming is a rapid reading technique we use to get a general idea of the topic and content of a text. It also helps the reader to identify the structure of a passage and locate various topics within the text. To skim a text, look for the key words and their synonyms (words with the same meaning). These are often repeated throughout the passage. The first sentence of a text usually indicates the main topic and the writer's focus.

Remember
At the beginning of the reading test, it is very important to spend five minutes *skimming* for the main topic and key ideas in the passage. This will help you later when you answer the questions.

1 Read the first sentence of each section of Reading Passage 1 and make a note of the key words and associated vocabulary.

A ....

B ....

C ....

D ....

E ....

F ....

2 Skim Reading Passage 1 and choose the most appropriate heading from the list below.

List of headings

A Nutrition and the international economy

B The planet's biggest killer

C A funding call for nutrition

D A new way of thinking about nutrition

For further practice in skimming refer to Listening Section 4, page 18.

A A new World Bank report warns unless action is taken within the first two years of a child's life to improve nutrition, children will suffer irreparable damage, ultimately adversely affecting the country's economic growth. The report, *Repositioning Nutrition as Central to Development*, says malnutrition remains the world's most serious health problem. Poor nutrition is implicated in more than half of all child deaths worldwide – a proportion unmatched by any infectious disease since the Black Death. 'Malnutrition is among the most serious health problems in the world today that has not been tackled,' says Meera Shekar, the report's lead author. 'Roughly 30% of children in the world are undernourished and in fact 60% of children for example who die of common diseases like malaria and diarrhea[1] would not have died had they not been malnourished in the first place.'

B While criticizing the lack of large-scale action internationally and within countries to tackle malnutrition, the report says improving nutrition could add two to three per cent to the growth rates of poor countries. And contrary to popular belief, it reveals the rates of malnutrition in South Asia are almost double those in Sub-Saharan Africa. 'We find the problem is much more severe in South Asia than in Sub-Saharan Africa. Roughly 50 per cent of children in South Asia are undernourished as compared to about 25 per cent in Sub-Saharan Africa. But we also find that the problem is not limited to those two regions alone. There are countries in other regions – Indonesia, Uzbekistan, Yemen, Guatemala and Peru – where the problem is acute as well.'

C The report dispels the notion that malnutrition is simply a problem for the world's poor countries. 'Poor nutrition also exists elsewhere, thus suggesting it's not simply a question of access to food,' Shekar says. 'India and Ethiopia have about the same levels of malnutrition. And 26 per cent of children in the highest income bracket in India are underweight and 65 per cent are anemic[2]. Anemic children perform less well in school, are more likely to drop out and have lower intellectual and physical productivity as adults. Everyone talks about how well India is doing in the IT industry – imagine how much better it could do if 65 per cent of the richest and 88 per cent of the poorest children were not anemic!' As Shekar says, the developed world also faces the other side of malnutrition – obesity. 'In the developed world, there's the other aspect of malnutrition that is coming up and that is the overweight agenda. And that links very closely to non-communicable disease like cardio-vascular heart disease, diabetes and cancers.'

[1] diarrhea = US spelling of *diarrhoea*
[2] anemic = US spelling of *anaemic*
[3] program = US spelling of *programme*
[4] center = US spelling of *centre*

D *Repositioning Nutrition as Central to Development* also dispels the notion that simply putting more food into the mouths of children can overcome malnutrition. It says actions targeted to older children have little, if any, effect on improving nutrition. The emphasis of any programs[3] to combat nutrition should therefore target pregnant women and children under two years of age. 'There is actually a very, very tight window of opportunity which is between conception through the first two years of life,' Shekar says. 'If we miss this window, we miss a whole generation. This is the time when the damage that happens due to malnutrition is in fact essentially irreparable damage. So if we had only one dollar to invest in improving nutrition that is where we would like to focus our actions. Many people assume that feeding children later in life will improve nutrition. Well, it's too little, too expensive and too late to improve nutrition or to improve future productivity.'

E Shekar says it's now time for the international community to re-think the importance it places on the value of nutrition. As the report says, 'the unequivocal choice now is between continuing to fail, as the global community did with HIV/AIDS for more than a decade, or to finally put nutrition at the center[4] of development so that a wide range of economic and social improvements that depend on nutrition can be realized.'

Shekar says in the past, the international community has thought of nutrition merely as a food consumption issue or a welfare issue. 'But the case we are making in this report is that nutrition is an investment issue. It is something that can drive economic growth rather than ride on the coat-tails of economic growth, because children who are well-nourished have been shown to have much higher income potential as adults.' The report makes the point that malnutrition is costing poor countries up to three per cent of their yearly GDP. And with the economies of many developing countries growing at a rate of two to three per cent annually, the report says improving nutrition could potentially double those rates.

F 'I think the biggest challenge now is getting the donor community to rally around this issue – to put resources, both technical and financial, behind this issue. And at the same time, there's a need to build commitment among government partners as well – to invest not only in nutrition but invest in the right kinds of things for nutrition.' The report calls on the donor community to co-finance a grant fund to jumpstart action in commitment-building and action research. Concurrently substantive funding is needed for developing countries through existing funding channels, to scale-up actions to prevent malnutrition.

Matching headings to paragraphs

This IELTS task type focuses on understanding the main idea of each section of the text. This can be done by skimming each part of the passage, and underlining key words and parallel expressions.

Reading Passage 1 has six sections **A–F**. Choose the most appropriate headings for sections **B–E** from the list below.

Remember
There are more headings than paragraphs in this type of question.
Although the first sentence of a paragraph is usually the topic sentence, look for more details to make sure you have understood the main ideas of the paragraph, which will be reflected in the heading.

List of headings
1   Nutrition and child mortality
2   Better nutrition means a more productive country
3   The failure of HIV/AIDS programmes
4   Comparing Asia and Africa
5   A problem for rich and poor
6   Effective programmes for the very young

B   ....
C   ....
D   ....
E   ....

Skills development

Scanning

Scanning is a reading technique that focuses on looking for details in a text, usually to answer a specific question. If you are looking for the context of the reading passage (who? where? when?), words with capital letters, dates and numbers are particularly useful and are easy to find in the text. However, you may be looking for exact meanings and the relationship between ideas. To do this you will focus not only on factual information, but also on words that link and relate ideas (eg *but*, *and*, *although*, *despite*).

Scanning for facts

Look at Sections **A**, **B** and **C** in Reading Passage 1 and complete the table below. If the exact information is not given, write **NG**.

Check your answers on page 101.

Area/country/continent	% of child population affected	
	anaemic	malnourished
1 world	NG	
2 South Asia		
3 Sub-Saharan Africa		
4 India/high income		
5 India/low income		

Multiple-choice questions

Remember
The key to answering these questions is finding the relevant part of the text quickly. If you are not sure which paragraph to check, choose a key word from the question and scan the text for it quickly.

With this type of question you will be able to use a combination of skimming and scanning. First you will skim the text to locate the relevant place and then read carefully to find the details you need to answer the question.

Circle the appropriate letters **A–D** to complete the sentences.

1   Malnutrition in Sub-Saharan Africa
   A   is less serious than in South Asia.
   B   is worse than in South Asia.
   C   results in more than 50% of child deaths.
   D   affects a quarter of the child population.

Tip
Scanning for names and
numbers can help you locate
the information you need
quickly.

Tip
There are other types of
multiple-choice questions.
For example, some ask you
to select from a list of four to
eight items the two or three
items which appear in the
text. Use skimming for gist
and scanning for detail to
answer them. Remember to
look out for synonyms and
paraphrases.

2 Shekar thinks the importance of nutrition must be reassessed because
   A it is as dangerous as HIV/AIDS.
   B it limits the success of a country's IT sector.
   C it is the most serious health problem in the world today.
   D it is the key to many economic and social improvements.

3 Shekar believes the biggest challenge in fighting malnutrition is
   A finding money.
   B reducing anaemia.
   C stopping obesity.
   D reducing child deaths.

Check your answers on page 101.

Skills development

Guessing meaning from context

There are almost always words in the text that will be unfamiliar to you. If you think the word is unimportant and doesn't affect your understanding of the text, ignore it. For example, the name of a person or a place beginning with a capital letter will not have a significant effect on the meaning of the text. However, the more frequently the word appears, the more important it is likely to be, and you may need to guess the meaning. One way to do this is to look at the words that surround it (the textual context). You may be able to find paraphrases of a word (alternative ways of expressing the same idea), or synonyms (different words with the same meaning) or even explanations and examples that make the meaning of the word clear.

Example: malnutrition

The more times a word appears in the text, the more clues there are about its meaning. The word nutrition appears in Section A of Reading Passage 1. As it appears many times in the text we know it's a key theme. The associated word *malnutrition* also occurs in Section A, where the words *poor nutrition* are used to mean the same thing. Other clues are: *most serious health problem*; and the information that poor nutrition in the first two years of a child's life causes irreparable damage. In Section C, we learn that one consequence of malnutrition is being underweight. Section D tells us that it takes more than just putting more food into children's mouths to overcome malnutrition. Given these clues, we can take a good guess at the meaning of malnutrition. The *Macmillan English Dictionary* says it is 'a medical condition in which you are weak or ill because you do not eat enough or you do not eat enough of the right foods'.

Look at the following words in their contexts and find clues about their meaning. Check your answers on page 101.

Section A	proportion
Section C	anaemic
Section C	obesity
Section F	funding

Skills practice

Now practise skimming, scanning and guessing the meaning of unfamiliar words by answering the questions on Reading Passage 2.

A Capital planning and priority-setting all tend to require that people reach agreement from different points of view. *Interest-based negotiation techniques* can help us focus our energy on the process, and guide that process toward a satisfactory result. By following these common-sense rules, we can turn conflict into cooperation, and reach solutions that work for everyone.

B If we view the problem as that which needs to be resolved rather than viewing someone holding a contrary viewpoint as a person to be defeated, the odds of a successful collaboration increase. Try changing the shape of the table rather than sitting opposite your 'opponents'. Arrange the seating so that all the parties are sitting together facing a flip chart or blackboard where the problem is presented. That makes it clear that all the participants are facing the problem together – that instead of it being 'us' against 'them', it is a case of 'all of us' against 'it'.

C Two sisters are fighting over the only orange in the family larder. Each sister must have the entire orange for herself; any less is impossible. A wise parent asks each of the girls (in private) why she wants the orange. One explains she wants to drink the juice; the other wants to use the rind to cook a pudding. What each sister wants is her *position*; why she wants it is her *interest*. In this case, the simple solution is to give the rind to the cook after the juice has been squeezed for the thirsty sister, thus meeting the interests of both.

When preparing for a negotiation, or after it has begun, don't just ask, 'What do they want?' It is also important to ask, 'Why do they want it?' It is equally important – but often more difficult – to ask the same questions about your own views. Many successful negotiators find they're more successful if they focus on understanding their interests as they enter discussions. If they haven't started out with a perfect package, the ideas of others may actually improve their final result. Negotiators who arrive with a complete package can create real problems. They may take personally and stubbornly resist any modifications to their ideas, making it more difficult to reach a satisfactory resolution.

D If you do not reach an agreement with the other party, does that really make things worse for you? When you're selling an antique Rolls Royce and have received an offer of $43,250, you know what another potential

buyer has to do to get you interested. Of course, the first offerer may plan to use the car for chauffeuring wedding parties, while a second offerer collects and restores antique cars and preserves them indoors. Is more cash all you care about, or is it important to you that your cherished Rolls is properly cared for? Or do you want to turn down both offers and keep the car for now? In determining your BATNA (Best Alternative to a Negotiated Agreement), a straightforward review of your interest will give you the clearest picture. If you accept your BATNA, you know when you can simply turn your back on the negotiations. But it is important not to ignore the other party's BATNA. The relative strength of each party's BATNA will determine the balance of power each can exercise.

E If the other party is highly opinionated or emotional, if their approach is threatening or extremely demanding, keeping quiet after they finish speaking can be quite unsettling to them. Most people are troubled by silence in the midst of heated discussion. Sometimes silence is viewed as disapproval. But since no specific disapproval has been voiced, it cannot be treated as an attack. It has happened on many occasions that, when met with silence, people have modified their previous statements to make them more palatable.

F If all the participants view the process as fair, they are more likely to take it seriously and 'buy into' its result. Moreover, the focus on fairness can have an important impact on the substantive result. If the parties to a negotiation can agree on standards against which elements of the agreement can be measured, it can give each a face saving reason for agreeing … . Parties who walk away from the table grumbling may regret their commitment and only honor it grudgingly. If they end up looking for excuses to get out from under an unwanted result, the gains achieved by the other side may prove to be short-term indeed.

G … keep a cool head and pay attention to the process and the strategy, as well as the substance of the negotiation. If it's not your 'turn' to be angry, the exercise of restraint can be turned into a positive opportunity to observe what is going on with a clear eye. No less important, yelling at each other is not negotiation; it is confrontation. In those situations there may possibly be a 'winner'; but it is even more likely there will be a 'loser'.

Question 1

Choose the most appropriate title for Reading Passage 2 from the list below.

> **List of titles**
> **A** Using BATNA
> **B** Fair negotiations
> **C** Getting the perfect package
> **D** Focusing negotiations on interests

Questions 2–7

Reading Passage 2 has seven sections **A–G**. Choose the most appropriate headings for sections **B–G** from the list below.

> **List of headings**
>   i   Wise parents
> ii   A fair agreement
> iii   Uniting people against the problem
> iv   Keeping your temper
>   v   Lawyers are expensive
> vi   Beating the opposition
> vii   Using silence to your advantage
> viii Distinguishing between interests and positions
> ix   Revising your interest

2   Section B ....
3   Section C ....
4   Section D ....

5   Section E ....
6   Section F ....
7   Section G ....

Questions 8–10

Circle the appropriate letters **A–D**.

8   The best way to start a negotiation is with
   A   a complete package of requirements.
   B   a completely open mind.
   C   everybody seated in a circle.
   D   a clear understanding of what you want and why you want it.

9   The purpose of a BATNA is
   A   to help you get more from the other party.
   B   to help you get more interest from your bank account.
   C   to help you decide when to stop the discussions.
   D   to help you get the best care for your car.

10 The effect of silence in negotiations can often be
   A   to make aggressive people uncomfortable.
   B   to threaten the other party.
   C   to help you calm down.
   D   to show disapproval.

Questions 11–13

Which **THREE** of the following statements does the writer make? Write the correct letter next to the question number.

A   People usually find important negotiations stressful.
B   In reducing conflict we should sometimes be ready to forget long-term objectives.
C   You need to defeat difficult people in negotiations.
D   A wise parent lets children argue until they are too tired to continue.
E   The other party may make good suggestions.
F   It may not be a big problem for you if the talks end with no agreement.
G   Experienced negotiators shouldn't get angry.

11 ....
12 ....
13 ....

Questions 14–16

Complete the following sentences using **ONE** word only from the text.

14 The writer uses the example of the two sisters to explain that a person's objective in a negotiation is their .... *interest* ....

15 The writer says that the reason why each sister wants their objective is their
.... *position* ....

16 An effective way to calm an animated argument is with .... *Negotiation* ....

Check your answers on page 102.

Reading Passage 3

Skills development

Summarizing and paraphrasing

When summarizing the main idea of a reading text it is important to be able to distinguish between main ideas and supporting ideas. By recognizing parallel expressions or paraphrases (words and phrases that express an original idea in different words) you will be able to decide whether an idea is being repeated or reinforced or whether a new idea is being introduced.

A way to practise recognizing paraphrases is to think of as many words and phrases as possible associated with key words in a text. Look at the following key words from sentence 1 of Section A, Reading Passage 3 and make a note of synonyms or associated words in the rest of Sections A and B.

1 ice cap   ....
2 disintegrate   ....
3 faster   ....
4 dramatically   ....

Check your answers on page 102.

Matching statements to paragraphs

This task type focuses on the ability to understand the main message of each section of the text. The following steps will help you:

- Identify the key words in the question. By reading the first sentence of each paragraph, you will usually be able to identify the main topic.
- Scan the rest of the paragraph for words and expressions that relate the main topic to the key words in the question.
- Look for details to decide which of the statements most accurately summarizes the main idea.

Questions 1–5

Reading Passage 3 has six sections **A–F**. Choose the most appropriate statements to summarize each section **A–E** from the list below.

> **List of statements**
> **i** Global sea levels are falling.
> **ii** Ice losses in Greenland depend on three factors.
> **iii** Sea levels may rise disastrously.
> **iv** As the ice sheet disintegrates sea levels will rise faster.
> **v** New glaciers are forming in Greenland.
> **vi** Glaciers are slow to form but quick to melt.
> **vii** Software predictions have underestimated the effects of crumbling glaciers.

1 Section A ....
2 Section B ....
3 Section C ....
4 Section D ....
5 Section E ....

Remember
By identifying synonyms and paraphrases throughout the text you will be able to:
- recognize the main ideas in each section;
- distinguish the main ideas from the supporting ideas or examples.

Remember
Skim the whole text and underline key points before trying to answer these questions.
Pay particular attention to the first sentence in each paragraph.

Tip
When two paragraphs seem to match a statement, scan the paragraphs again for similar ideas and parallel expressions to those in the statement and underline them. Read those sentences carefully to help you choose.

Question 6
Choose the most appropriate title for Reading Passage 3 from the list below.

List of titles
A The end of the Greenland ice sheet
B Ice sheet melt raises sea levels faster than forecast
C Catastrophe at sea level in Greenland
D The history of Greenland

Reading Passage 3

A Global warming is causing the Greenland ice cap to disintegrate far faster than anyone predicted. A study of the region's massive ice sheet warns that sea levels may – as a consequence – rise more dramatically than expected. Scientists have found that many of the huge glaciers of Greenland are moving at an accelerating rate – dumping twice as much ice into the sea as five years ago – indicating that the ice sheet is undergoing a potentially catastrophic breakup. The implications of the research are dramatic given Greenland holds enough ice to raise global sea levels by up to 21 feet[1], a disaster scenario that would result in the flooding of some of the world's major population centres, including all of Britain's city ports. Satellite measurements of the entire land mass of Greenland show that the speed at which the glaciers are moving to the sea has increased significantly over the past ten years with some glaciers moving three times faster than in the mid-1990s.

B Scientists believe that computer models of how the Greenland ice sheet will react to global warming have seriously underestimated the threat posed by sea levels that could rise far more quickly than envisaged. The latest study, presented at the American Association for the Advancement of Science in St Louis, shows that rather than just melting relatively slowly, the ice sheet is showing all the signs of a mechanical breakup as glaciers slip ever faster into the ocean, aided by the 'lubricant' of melt water forming at their base.

C Eric Rignot, a scientist at the Jet Propulsion Laboratory and the California Institute of Technology in Pasadena, said that computer models used by the UN's International Panel on Climate Change have not adequately taken into account the amount of ice falling into the sea from glacial movements. Yet the satellite study shows that about two-thirds of the sea-level rise caused by the Greenland ice sheet is due to icebergs breaking off from fast-moving glaciers rather than simply the result of water running off from melting ice. 'In simple terms, the ice sheet is breaking up rather than melting. It's not a surprise in itself but it is a surprise to see the magnitude of the changes. These big glaciers seem to be accelerating, they seem to be going faster and faster to the sea,' Dr Rignot said. 'This is not predicted by the current computer models. The fact is the glaciers of Greenland are evolving faster than we thought and the models have to be adjusted to catch up with these observations,' he said.

[1] 21 feet = approx 6.4 metres

D The Greenland ice sheet covers an area of 1.7 million sq km – about the size of Mexico – and, in places, is up to 3km thick. It formed over thousands of years by the gradual accumulation of ice and snow but now its disintegration could occur in decades or centuries. Over the past 20 years, the air temperature of Greenland has risen by 3°C and computer models suggested it would take at least 1,000 years for the ice sheet to melt completely. But the latest study suggests that glaciers moving at an accelerating rate could bring about a much faster change. 'The behaviour of the glaciers that dump ice into the sea is the most important aspect of understanding how an ice sheet will evolve in a changing climate,' Dr Rignot said. 'It takes a long time to build and melt an ice sheet but glaciers can react quickly to temperature changes. Climate warming can work in different ways but, generally speaking, if you warm up the ice sheet, the glacier will flow faster,' he said.

E The ice 'balance sheet' of Greenland is complex but – in simple terms – it depends on the amount of snow that falls, the amount of ice that melts as run-off and the amount of ice that falls directly into the sea in the form of icebergs 'calving' from moving glaciers.

Satellites show that the glaciers in the south of Greenland are now moving much faster than they were ten years ago. Scientists estimate that, in 1996, glaciers deposited about 50 cubic km of ice into the sea. In 2005 it had risen to 150 cubic km of ice. Details of the latest study, published in the journal *Science*, show that Greenland now accounts for an increase in global sea levels of about 0.5 millimetres per year – compared to a total sea level rise of 3mm per year. When previous studies of the ice balance are taken into account, the researchers calculated that the overall amount of ice dumped into the sea increased from 90 cubic km in 1996 to 224 cubic km in 2005.

F Dr Rignot said that there are now signs that the more northerly glaciers of Greenland are beginning to adopt the pattern of movements seen by those in the south. 'The southern half of Greenland is reacting to what we think is climate warming. The northern half is waiting, but I don't think it's going to take long,' he said.

Skills development

Scanning for opinions

> **Tip**
> Remember that you may not see the same word in the text – you may need to look for synonyms.

Scanning for opinions is useful when you are asked to identify the point of view of a writer or person mentioned in the text. When you are looking for opinions, scan for specific words eg *think*, *state*, *view*, *comment*, *believe*.

1 Before you answer questions **7–12**, scan the text for the following words and match them to the correct people or organizations.

1	Section A	*have found*	....
2	Section B	*believe*	....
3	Section C	*said*	....
4	Section C	*thought*	....
5	Section D	*suggests*	....
6	Section E	*estimate*	....
7	Section E	*calculated*	....

Check your answers on page 102.

Questions 7–12

Put the correct letter **A–C** next to questions **7–12**.

The following views and information are given by:

A scientists
B the most recent report on the Greenland ice sheet
C Eric Rignot

7 Glaciers react very quickly to temperature variations.   ....
8 If glaciers move more quickly, sea levels could rise much more rapidly.   ....
9 Predictions have miscalculated the speed at which sea levels will rise.   ....
10 Between 1996 and 2005 the amount of ice deposited into the sea
   increased from 50–150 cubic km.   ....
11 Calculations have not included the ice that falls into the sea as icebergs. ....
12 The northern part of Greenland is going to behave in the same way
   as the south.   ....

Check your answers on page 102.

2 When you are asked to find specific, detailed information in a text, you first need to identify the key words in the question. You should then find them in the text. Look at the statements in questions **13** and **14** and underline the key words.

Check your answers on page 102.

Questions 13–14

Which **TWO** of the following statements are mentioned by the writer?

A Glaciers in the southern hemisphere are disappearing more quickly than those in the north.
B Glaciers in Greenland have started to flow much more quickly towards the sea over the past ten years.
C Nearly all the sea ports around the world would disappear under water if all the world's glaciers melted.
D Glaciers provide an important habitat for some bacteria and animals.
E More than half the rise in sea level is caused by glaciers breaking up, not melting.

13 ....
14 ....

Check your answers on page 102.

Questions 15–17
Complete the sentences below with words from Reading Passage 3. Write **ONE WORD** for each answer.

15 The melt water around the base of glaciers reaching the sea acts as a
   .... which aids their breakup.
16 An essential factor in understanding the effect of climate change on ice sheets is
   the .... of glaciers.
17 Although the Greenland ice sheet took many millennia to develop, its
   .... could take place in a matter of decades.

Check your answers on page 102.

True/False/Not given

Questions 18–22

Do the following statements agree with the information given in Reading Passage 3?

Write:

TRUE   if the statement is true according to the passage
FALSE   if the statement is false according to the passage
NOT GIVEN if there is no information about this

18 Some of Greenland's biggest glaciers are depositing three times as much ice into the sea as five years ago.
19 Scientists believe that past predictions about the Greenland ice sheet are more or less accurate.
20 The glaciers of Greenland were gradually formed by snow and ice.
21 There are three main ways in which global warming can affect crops.
22 Scientists believe that in the year 2000, glaciers deposited about 100 cubic km of ice into the ocean.

Check your answers on page 102.

Reading Passage 4

Skills practice

Now practise summarizing, paraphrasing and scanning for detail and opinion, by answering questions 1–20 from Reading Passage 4.

Questions 1–5

Reading Passage 4 has ten paragraphs lettered **A–J**. Which paragraph contains the following information? Write the letters **A–J** by the question numbers.

i   Vegetarians think more carefully about what they eat, but research has not established the reason why intelligent children choose to become vegetarians.
ii   Clever children often become vegetarian adults, which may be the reason why fewer intelligent people suffer from heart disease.
iii The health advantages of vegetarianism may include reduced cholesterol levels and lower blood pressure.
iv Because intelligent people suffer less from coronary disease, researchers have been investigating whether there is a connection between vegetarianism and intelligence.
v   Although vegetarians tend to be more educated, they are not necessarily better off materially.

1 ....
2 ....
3 ....
4 ....
5 ....

Now check your answers on page 102.

Tip
As you read the passage, <u>underline</u> the part that answers the questions. If you cannot <u>underline</u> it, the answer is probably **NOT GIVEN**.

A It's official – vegetarians really are smarter. But it is not because of what they eat. Bright children are more likely to reject meat and opt to become vegetarians when they grow up, a study has shown. Clever veggies are born not made.

B The finding helps explain how a team of vegetarians won the BBC Test the Nation competition in September, when they beat off competition from six other teams including butchers, public school pupils and footballers' wives to achieve the highest overall IQ score.

C The top scoring individual in the contest, Marie Bidmead, 68, a mother of five from Churcham, Gloucester, was also a vegetarian. 'I think it shows we veggies are good thinkers. We think about what we eat for a start,' she said.

D Researchers from the University of Southampton who conducted the study agree. They suggest that vegetarians are more thoughtful about what they eat. But they say it is unclear whether bright children choose to become vegetarians for the health benefits or for other reasons, such as a concern for animals, or as a lifestyle choice.

E The scientists began investigating the link between IQ and vegetarianism because people with higher intelligence have a lower risk of heart disease, which has long puzzled doctors.

F A vegetarian diet is associated with a lower cholesterol level, lower blood pressure and less obesity – all risk factors for heart disease. The researchers wondered if this could explain the health advantage of having a high IQ. They cite Benjamin Franklin, the 18th-century statesman and scientist, who said that a vegetarian diet results in a 'greater clearness of head and quicker comprehension'. He may not have realised that this was because of whom was eating rather than what was eaten.

G However, early last century doctors were less enamoured of the practice. Robert Hutchison told the British Medical Association in 1930: 'Vegetarianism is harmless enough though it is apt to fill a man with wind and self-righteousness.'

H The study, published in the British Medical Journal, was based on more than 8,000 people born in 1970 whose IQ was measured at age 10. Now aged 36, the researchers found 366, just under one in 20, said they were vegetarians (a third of these ate chicken or fish but none touched red meat).

I As well as being brighter, the vegetarians were better educated and of higher social class but the link with intelligence remained statistically significant even after adjusting for these factors. Despite their intelligence they were not wealthier and more likely to be working for charities or in education. 'It may be that ethical considerations determined not just their diet but also their choice of employment,' the report said.

J It concludes: 'Our finding that children with greater intelligence are more likely to report being vegetarian as adults, coupled with the evidence on the potential health benefits of a vegetarian diet, may help to explain why higher IQ in childhood or adolescence is linked with a reduced risk of coronary heart disease in adult life.'

The benefits of forsaking meat

- A vegetarian diet tends to be lower in fat, higher in fibre and vitamins
- Vegetarian diets are associated with lower cholesterol, lower blood pressure, and less obesity
- Vegetarians have lower rates of heart disease, less diabetes and may have less risk of cancer and dementia
- The Vegetarian Society, claimed to be the oldest in the world, was founded in Ramsgate, Kent, in 1847. Mahatma Gandhi, George Bernard Shaw and Linda McCartney were members
- 'Vegetarian' is derived from the Latin vegetus, meaning 'lively' and was intended to be suggestive of the English 'vegetable'

Question 6

Skim through Reading Passage 4 and choose the most appropriate title from the list below.

List of titles
A Vegetarianism and heart disease
B Linking intelligence and vegetarianism
C Intelligence and health
D Vegetarians are more successful

Questions 7–10

Complete sentences **7–10** with words from Reading Passage 4. Write **NO MORE THAN THREE** words for each answer.

7 It is generally believed that vegetarians are better .... than meat-eaters.

8 Some people become vegetarian because they believe it is beneficial for their
....

9 High .... and cholesterol levels are two of the causes of heart disease.

10 People who choose to be vegetarians may do so for .... reasons.

Questions 11–12

Which **TWO** of the following statements are made by the writer? Write letters **A–E** by the question numbers.

A Benjamin Franklin was a vegetarian.
B According to the British Medical Journal, some of the vegetarians in the study ate white meat and seafood.
C Better educated adults are usually vegetarians.
D Vegetarians have more highly developed cognitive powers.
E Vegetarianism increases intelligence.

11 ....
12 ....

Questions 13–17

Complete the summary below. Choose **NO MORE THAN TWO WORDS** from Reading Passage 4 for each answer.

Research has found that intelligent children have a tendency to prefer a
(13) .... As vegetarians think more carefully about what they consume, they eat (14) .... and more (15) ....
than meat eaters. This (16) .... results in lower blood pressure and cholesterol levels, and reduces the incidence of obesity. As a result of their research scientists have been able to make a connection between higher intelligence levels and lower occurrences of (17) ....

Questions 18–20

Read the text and answer these questions. Write **NO MORE THAN THREE WORDS AND/OR A NUMBER** for each answer.

18 How many of the people in the study were vegetarian at the age of 36?
....

19 In which professions do vegetarians often work?
....

20 When was vegetarianism unpopular with the medical profession?
....

Now check your answers on page 102.

Identifying and comparing data on a chart

Some texts include statistics and data in graphical form. To understand this information, first identify:

- the title of the chart
- the title of each axis (horizontal and vertical)
- the label of each category, represented by a column, row or line in the chart
- the units of measurement for each axis (eg time, numbers, percentages, distances)
- the values for each category
- the legend (the colour or pattern assigned to each category in the chart)

1 Look at the chart below and answer the following questions:

i   What is the title of the chart?
ii Suggest a title for the vertical axis.
iii What is the unit of measurement on the horizontal axis?

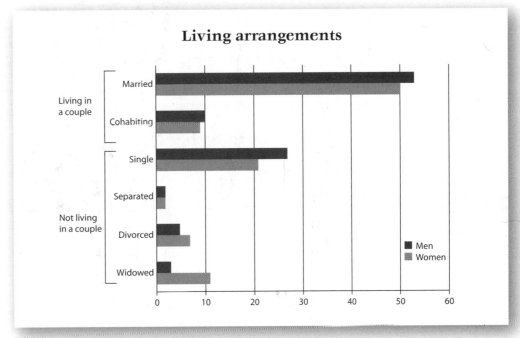

Source: UK National Statistics.

Check your answers on page 102.

2 Read the following text which describes some of the information in the chart above. Using words from the text complete the summary below. Write **NO MORE THAN TWO WORDS OR A NUMBER** in each space.

> Despite the decrease in the numbers of people marrying, marriage remains the main type of partnership for men and women in Great Britain. In 2004/05 around half of men and women were married and one in ten were cohabiting. The average age at which people get married for the first time in England and Wales has risen by more than six and a half years over the last three decades, to 31 for men and 29 for women in 2004.

Summary

In 2004, of the 60 per cent of the population living in a (1) .... only (2) .... per cent were unmarried. Men and women typically married for the first time at (3) .... and (4) .... respectively, which is over six and a half years later than in (5) ....

Check your answers with the key on page 102.

Identifying and following the argument in a text

To follow the key ideas in a text:
- skim each paragraph to identify the main topic. This is usually in the first sentence of the paragraph.

To identify the topic of each part of the text:
- scan for paraphrases of the main topic.

To identify the relationship between the ideas scan for:
- time phrases, dates and words of sequence (like: *first, second, then, finally, after…*) that identify chronological developments, processes or contrasting periods of time.
- words that indicate contrast, addition, cause and effect, similarity and condition like: *but, and, however, in spite of, so, therefore*.
- Verb tenses and phrases and that indicate: completed events, current events and plans or suggestions. For example: *has become …, are -ing, have been -ing, there will be …*.

Skills development

Summary

Reading Passage 5

1 Read sections **A–D** in Reading Passage 5 and choose the most appropriate title from the list below.

List of titles

A Single women outnumber men
B Marriage is no longer popular
C Number of single women hits all time high
D Wives lose out to single women
E 11 million new marriages

Now check your answer on page 102.

Reading Passage 5

A Married women are outnumbered by singletons for the first time, official figures show.

B There are more single, divorced and widowed women than wives in England and Wales according to the Office for National Statistics.

C The figures in the latest edition of Population Trends show that unmarried women became the majority in 2004.

D Between 1996 and 2004 the number of divorced and single women rose by 1.5 million. Fewer than 11 million are now married.

Marriage has become particularly unfashionable for women in their 20s. Perhaps mindful of the divorce statistics, couples are waiting longer than ever before making a commitment to marriage.

In the early 1970s, 85 per cent of women were married before their 30th birthday. Now fewer than one in three women in her late 20s is married. The ONS figures showed than in 2003 there were 11 million wives compared with 10,892,000 single, divorced or widowed women.

In 2004, married women fell to 10,935,000 while single, divorced or widowed women rose to 11,090,000. Marriage projections have great implications for government policy, as well as significant sociological effects. For example, if current trends continue, there will be far fewer hefty divorce settlements in favour of women.

The number of cohabiting couples is projected to rise from two million to 3.8 million in 2031 and they will also be older on average.

The number of people living together at the age of 45 to 64 is projected to rise to 1.25 million men in 2031, compared with 375,000 in 2003, and from 317,000 to more than 1.1 million women.

Jill Kirby, of the Centre for Policy Studies, said: 'The serious decline of marriage is a very worrying development. Cohabitation is an inherently fragile partnership.

It is not divorce that will have a serious impact on children in the future but parents moving in and out of different relationships in which marriage is not a factor. A lot of women in their forties and fifties will be living alone, perhaps having had a relationship or two but never having been married, with all sorts of emotional and financial implications.'

The trend away from marriage is similar to the US where married couples – whose numbers have been declining for decades as a proportion of American households – finally slipped into a minority, according to a recent analysis of new census figures by The New York Times.

The American Community Survey, by the Census Bureau, found that 49.7 per cent, or 55.2 million, of the nation's 111.1 million households in 2005 were made up of married couples – with and without children – down from more than 52 per cent five years earlier.

Experts said the decision not to marry was partially fuelled by women in the work force who do not necessarily have to marry to be economically secure.

Andrew Beveridge, a demographer at Queens College of the City University of New York, said: 'You used to get married to have sex. Now one of the major reasons to get married is to have children, and the attractiveness of having children has declined for many people because of the cost.'

The Fawcett Society, which campaigns for equality of the sexes, said: 'In some respects, home and family life is very different for women now compared to the 1970s.

The percentage of married women has dropped from 74 per cent in 1979 to 49 per cent. The average number of children per household has gone down from two in 1971 to 1.8 in 2001. Instead, many more couples cohabit.

But it is striking how little has changed at home for many women. While we have had a revolution in the large numbers of women going out to work, men still are not sharing the unpaid work in the home.

We now need a revolution in men's lives too. This would be of benefit not only to women with male partners, but to all women and men who want a better work–life balance.'

Synonyms

2 Complete each column below by scanning Reading Passage 5 for synonyms (words with the same meaning), antonyms (opposites) and phrases associated with the following words.

Married women	Cohabitation
synonyms wives	synonyms
antonyms	antonyms
associated expressions	associated expressions

Check your answers on page 103.

Scanning for detail

3 By scanning the text for time phrases you can trace the sequence of events and identify when the passage is comparing past and present situations or describing events that have happened over a period of time.

Scan Reading Passage 5 and match the statistics **A–G** with the time they happened or are predicted to happen, **1–7**.

Check your answers on page 103.

1	in the early 1970s	A	1.8 children per household
2	in 2004	B	49.7 per cent married couples in US
3	in 2031	C	52 per cent married couples in US
4	in 2005	D	2 children per household
5	in 2000	E	fewer than 11 million married women
6	in 2001	F	85 per cent of women married under 30
7	in 1971	G	nearly 4 million unmarried partnerships

4 In this exercise you will practice locating expressions that indicate contrast, possibility and cause and effect. Write true (T), false (F) or not given (NG) by the following statements.

1 Couples may be marrying later because they are concerned about the high rate of divorce. ....
2 Men will have to pay larger divorce settlements if fewer women marry. ....
3 Cohabitation is as stable a partnership as marriage. ....
4 In the future, short-term relationships between parents will have a more detrimental effect on children than divorce. ....
5 Women who are financially independent are having more children. ....
6 Couples are less inclined to have children because they are very expensive to raise. ....
7 Although women work more outside the home, they still do the majority of the housework. ....
8 Men have a better work–life balance than women. ....

Check your answers on page 103.

5 When you read texts that include figures and statistics, it is important to identify how the different items of information relate to each other. You can do this by scanning for words like: *between/compared with/rise/risen/down/up from/to/fewer than, more than.*

Complete the sentences below with information from Reading Passage 5 and the correct linking word or phrase from the list above.

Example: There are *fewer* married women than single women.

1 In 1971, 85 per cent of women married under 30 .... 30 per cent in 2005.
2 By 2031 the number of men aged .... 45 and 64 who cohabit is expected to .... to 1.25 million.
3 In 2031 .... women than men are predicted to be living with a partner.
4 The number of married couples in the United States in 2005 is .... that of 2000.
5 The percentage of single women in the United States has .... since 1979.

Check your answers on page 103.

Skills practice

Now practise skimming for key words, scanning for detail, locating specific information in the text and following the argument by answering questions **1–15** from Reading Passage 6.

Multiple-choice questions

Questions 1–5

Circle the appropriate letters **A–D**.

1   Most newspapers in industrialized countries are losing income because
   A   their machinery is out of date.
   B   people have stopped reading the news.
   C   they still rely on print to make a profit.
   D   they are advertising on the internet.

2   Advertising in print has
   A   increased progressively over the years.
   B   maintained its position in relation to the internet.
   C   become popular with young people.
   D   lost its percentage of the advertising market.

3   In order to stay in business newspapers are
   A   expanding into the multimedia market.
   B   selling mobile phones.
   C   waiting to see what happens.
   D   copying their print editions onto the internet.

4   It was a mistake for newspapers to use novice writers in the early days of online journalism because
   A   the more experienced journalists shared their ideas with them.
   B   their writing was of a low standard.
   C   their articles were copied onto other websites.
   D   they copied their material from other journalists.

5   These days many newspapers recognize the importance of their online editions by
   A   making print journalists work with online writers.
   B   employing cheaper staff.
   C   giving reporters time to think carefully about their writing.
   D   keeping print and website writers in different departments.

More media, less news

1 The first thing to greet a visitor to the Oslo headquarters of Schibsted, a Norwegian newspaper firm, is its original, hand-operated printing press from 1856, now so clean and polished it looks more like a sculpture than a machine. Christian Schibsted, the firm's founder, bought it to print someone else's newspaper, but when the contract moved elsewhere he decided to start his own. Although Schibsted gives pride of place to its antique machinery, the company is in fact running away from its printed past as fast as it can. Having made a loss five years ago, Schibsted's activities on the internet contributed 35% of last year's operating profits.

2 Unfortunately for the newspaper industry, Schibsted is a rare exception. For most newspaper companies in the developed world, 2005 was miserable. They still earn almost all of their profits from print, which is in decline. As people look to the internet for news and young people turn away from papers, paid-for circulations are falling year after year. Papers are also losing their share of advertising spending. Classified advertising is quickly moving online. Jim Chisholm, of iMedia, a joint-venture consultancy with IFRA, a newspaper trade association, predicts that a quarter of print classified ads will be lost to digital media in the next ten years. Overall, says iMedia, newspapers claimed 36% of total global advertising in 1995 and 30% in 2005. It reckons they will lose another five percentage points by 2015.

3 Even the most confident of newspaper bosses now agree that they will survive in the long term only if, like Schibsted, they can reinvent themselves on the internet and on other new-media platforms such as mobile phones and portable electronic devices. Most have been slow to grasp the changes affecting their industry– 'remarkably, unaccountably complacent', as Rupert Murdoch put it in a speech last year–but now they are making a big push to catch up. Internet advertising is growing rapidly for many and is beginning to offset some of the decline in print.

4 At first, from the late 1990s until around 2002, newspaper companies simply replicated their print editions online. Yet the internet offers so many specialised sources of information and entertainment that readers can pick exactly what they want from different websites. As a result, people visited newspaper sites infrequently, looked at a few pages and then vanished off to someone else's website.

Another early mistake was for papers to save their best journalists for print. This meant that the quality of new online editions was often poor. Websites hired younger, cheaper staff. The brand's prestige stayed with the old medium, which encouraged print journalists to defend their turf. Still today at *La Stampa*, an Italian daily paper owned by the Fiat Group, says Anna Masera, the paper's internet chief, print journalists hesitate to give her their stories for fear that the website will cannibalise the newspaper.

5 For the past couple of years, however, newspapers have been thinking more boldly about what to do on the internet. At its most basic, that means reporting stories using cameras and microphones as well as print.

More newspaper companies are likely to treat their websites as a priority these days. 'Before, newspapers used their second- and third-rate journalists for the internet,' says Edward Roussel, online editorial director at Britain's Telegraph Group, 'but now we know we've got to use our very best'. Many companies are putting print journalists in the same room as those who work online, so that print writers are working for the website and vice versa. Some insist that this is a mistake. 'It is completely wrong not to separate web and paper operations,' says Oscar Bronner, publisher of *Der Standard*, a daily paper in Austria. Print journalists don't have time to reflect and analyse properly if they also have to work for the website, he argues.

6 How impressive are the results of these online experiments? At lots of newspaper companies, internet advertising is growing by at least 30% a year, and often more. At *la Repubblica* in Italy, for instance, the paper's website gets about 1m visitors a day, nearly double the circulation of the printed paper. The value of online ads grew by 70% in the first half of 2006. For the first three months of 2006, the Newspaper Association of America announced that advertising for all the country's newspaper websites grew by 35% from the same period in 2005, to a total of $613m. But to put that in perspective, print and online ads together grew by only 1.8%, to $11 billion, because print advertising was flat. At almost all newspapers the internet brings in less than a tenth of revenues and profits. At this point, says Mr Chisholm, 'Newspapers are halfway to realising an audience on the internet and about a tenth of the way to building a business online.'

Completing sentences

Questions 6–9

Complete sentences **6–9** with words from Reading Passage 6. Write **NO MORE THAN THREE WORDS** for each answer.

6 .... in the Italian newspaper *la Repubblica* increased by 70 per cent between January and June 2006.

7 Traditional business still represents more than 90 per cent of newspaper ....

8 Some of the loss of income from print newspapers is being compensated by .... advertising.

9 Early online editions failed to understand that readers could choose from a range of .... specializing in news and entertainment.

Identifying the writer's point of view

Questions that ask you to *identify the views of the writer* of the passage will give you the option of selecting:

YES	when the statement agrees with the writer's views
NO	when the statement disagrees with the writer's views
NOT GIVEN	when the writer's point of view is not clearly stated

Questions 10–13

Do the following statements agree with the views of the writer in Reading Passage 6?

Write:

YES	if the statement agrees with the views of the writer
NO	if the statement disagrees with the views of the writer
NOT GIVEN	if it is not possible to say what the writer thinks about this

10 The newspaper industry would benefit if it had a larger number of visionary executives.

11 Print journalists should avoid giving their stories to their editors to put on the website.

12 Newspapers should replace print with online video recordings.

13 Although internet advertising is increasing it is still a very small part of the proceeds of the newspaper business.

Questions 14–15

From the information in Reading Passage 6, select a label to identify A and B in the diagram below.

List of labels
i print advertising
ii online advertising
iii print and online sales
iv print and online advertising

14 A ....

15 B ....

Check your answers on page 103.

Skills development

In this exercise you will practise distinguishing fact from opinion. You will need to know whether information given in a text is objective, or the point of view of the writer or the people mentioned in the text.

To identify *facts* in a text, look for: data, statistics, dates and places. Also look for verbs **without** modifiers (eg *may, should, could*) or adverbs such as *maybe, perhaps*.

Opinions, on the other hand, are identified by *modal verbs (may, might, should)*, *adjectives* and words of reflection and feeling (*think, feel, imagine, surprise*).

Underline the modal verbs in Section B and match them with the opinions below.

i ....
ii ....
iii ....
iv ....

A Our understanding of our religious needs has altered since we lived in primitive societies.
B Our religious practices are probably different from those of our ancestors.
C It is fairly predictable that architecture should not have changed, as it fulfils our most fundamental need for shelter.
D Some people consider that architecture has remained substantially the same over the last six millennia.

Check your answers on page 103.

True/False/Not given questions

Questions 1–5

Do the following statements agree with the information in Reading Passage 7?

Write:

TRUE   if the statement agrees with the information given
FALSE   if the statement contradicts the information given
NOT GIVEN   if there is no information about this

1 Human beings have been on this planet for about 300,000 years. ....
2 The first homes human beings made were tents. ....
3 Before making their own homes, human beings lived in caves. ....
4 The main change in architecture, for thousands of years, was simply the number of structures built. ....
5 The ancient Romans constructed buildings of over ten stories. ....

> **Tip**
> Before checking your answers on page 103, underline the source of information in the text for questions 1–5.
> If you cannot find the correct words to underline, the answer is probably **NOT GIVEN**.

> **Remember**
> For each statement, locate the relevant part of the text. Only write **TRUE** or **FALSE** if the statements agree with or contradict information in the text. If the text contains no clear information about the statement, write **NOT GIVEN**. The question and the text may use different words.

> **Tip**
> Since these questions focus on *details*, it may be helpful to answer them after you have answered questions about the *general* meaning of the passage.

The Beginning of Architecture

A Compared to other human activities, architecture is a young art that had its beginnings only 10,000 years ago when men and women, having discovered agriculture and husbandry, were able to give up roaming the surface of the earth in search of food. Until then they had been exposed to the weather, precariously protected by tents of animal skins. Perpetually on the move, they cooked over campfires and gathered in small tribes.

All of this changed when people became sedentary. Tents were supplanted by more substantial abodes, and a permanent hearth became the center of the home. Numerous huts sprang up in fertile areas; contact between families became more frequent and intimate; villages grew. From village to village a network of paths was worn. At times paths had to cross rivers and ravines, requiring the construction of footbridges made out of tree trunks or suspended from ropes of vegetable fibers.

The clustering of huts created the need for larger huts where village problems could be discussed. These larger structures served both as town halls and churches, since spiritual needs have always gone hand in hand with the physical. Indeed the larger monuments of archeological architecture were often motivated by spiritual needs.

B The last ten thousand years spanned more than 300 generations, but we who have witnessed the incredible changes brought to our cultures by the Industrial Revolution may feel that architecture has not changed much, at least over the last 6,000 years. This constancy in the built environment should not surprise us, if we realize that architecture satisfies basic physiological needs, which have not changed since *Homo sapiens* appeared about 3 million years ago. We eat the same kinds of food as our prehistoric ancestors, and we cook food much as they did. We sleep on horizontal surfaces (though surely softer today than then), we protect ourselves from the weather, and we procreate in the only way we can. Architecture is the most conservative of the human arts and sciences because it caters to these unchanging needs of man. Even our spiritual needs, which may have changed somewhat and may have produced different rituals, are as basic today as they were in prehistory.

C Changes in architecture, more quantitative than qualitative, have been motivated by the conglomeration of people. The city is a friend to architecture. Whether we gathered first in villages, and then towns and cities, the better to defend ourselves from enemies, or whether the exchange of trades and crafts required the proximity of first hundreds, and eventually millions, it was the city that led us to erect taller and taller buildings and to enclose larger and larger spaces. In 2000 B.C. Minoan cities on Crete already boasted four-story houses, and tenements in the most popular sections of Rome had risen as high as ten stories.

We are the heirs of these builders. We think of ourselves as the most individualistic human beings in history and yet we gather in large halls to see the same spectacles and live in beehives containing hundreds of identical apartments. Nostalgic as we may be for the simple life of the forest, most of us find the ways of the city more congenial and more efficient. By the year 2000 twenty cities, most of them in Latin America and Southeast Asia, had concentrated 20 or more million people in small areas. We have become members of group cultures. The relative isolation of the countryside is no longer our way of life.

D Science and technology at their best are motivated to satisfy genuine human needs. If architecture has never changed much in its functional aspects, it has undergone a fantastic technical revolution. The needs of the city will be satisfied, and technology, spurred by the discoveries and inventions of the industrial and scientific revolutions, has come to help.

It may be surprising to realize that such a highly technological field has contributed so much to our innate need for beauty. To those of us who cannot live without beauty, this is an encouraging thought. The separation of art and technology is both unnecessary and incorrect; one is not an enemy of the other. Instead it is essential to understand that technology is often a necessary component of art and that art helps technology to serve man better. Nowhere is this more true than in architecture and structure, a marriage in which science and beauty combine to fulfil some of the most basic and spiritual needs of humanity.

Summary completion

Before completing the summary, first identify and <u>underline</u> the key points of the text. Practise by skimming the first sentence of each section and matching sections **A–D** with headings **1–6**.

A ....
B ....
C ....
D ....

> **List of headings**
> 1 Art and science should complement each other.
> 2 In architecture, technology is more important than design.
> 3 Most city dwellers would prefer to live in the forest.
> 4 Architecture and villages originated with early farm settlements.
> 5 There has been no fundamental change in architecture since 4000 B.C.
> 6 Architecture has developed in density since cities were founded.

Check your answers on page 103.

Questions 6–10

Complete the summary of paragraphs **4–6** below. Choose **NO MORE THAN TWO WORDS** from Reading Passage 7 for each answer.

Viewed historically (6) .... has changed very little during the last 6,000 years. There are several basic reasons for this; for example, human beings still need shelter from (7) .... Over the years, cities developed from a need for people to (8) .... themselves from hostile outsiders and to (9) .... goods. These factors, amongst others, have brought people together in progressively larger communities. The development of cities has led, more recently, to the construction of higher (10) ....

Check your answers on page 103.

Pictures and diagrams

Tip
In some questions you will match pictures to the labels provided. In others, you will have to find the correct words in the text to complete a diagram.

Remember
First scan for figures, key words or their synonyms. Then read more carefully to identify the relationships between the figures and the ideas.

Some IELTS questions require you to transfer information from a written text to a picture, chart or diagram. In these cases you will need to read for specific, detailed information. This may take the form of numbers or percentages or it may describe a process. If the diagram is based on numerical information, you will scan the text for the relevant figures. When you are asked to complete a diagram describing a process, you will need to look for words that express sequence or the development of an event over a period of time. (See 'Identifying and following the argument in a text', page 36.)

Taking your information from Reading Passage 7, complete the diagram with the letters **A–F**.

A As time passed, communities grew larger to provide better protection and more effective trade.
B More recent technological developments have allowed cities to both increase in density and become aesthetically pleasing.
C When people settled down to cultivate crops they lived in groups of huts.
D Initially, early tribes travelled from place to place living in tents.
E Subsequently, primitive roads were trodden between villages.
F As communities developed, they constructed larger buildings for social gatherings.

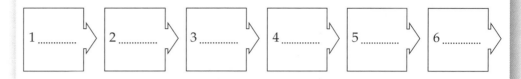

6 development stages in man's move from 'nomadic existence in tents to cities and urban communities'

1 .... ▷ 2 .... ▷ 3 .... ▷ 4 .... ▷ 5 .... ▷ 6 .... ▷

Check your answers on page 103.

Skills practice

Reading Passage 8

Now practise distinguishing fact from opinion and looking for detailed information by answering questions **1–6** on Reading Passage 8.

Questions 1–6

Do the following statements agree with the information given in Reading Passage 8?

Write:

TRUE	if the statement agrees with the information in the text
FALSE	if the statement contradicts the information in the text
NOT GIVEN	if the text contains no information about the statement

1 There has been a serious decline in technological development in recent years.
2 Illegal wireless networks are attached to over a third of US corporation systems.
3 It is common for companies to give authorized network access to visitors.
4 It is not possible to create software that protects hand-held computers against viruses.
5 The latest security model allows people to use networks under controlled conditions.
6 Hackers often use unauthorized wireless network access points.

Tip
You can do the questions in any order. You may like to do the questions that help your general comprehension before you do the questions that ask you to find detailed information.

Reading Passage 8

A Wireless networking, using the so-called Wi-Fi [1] protocol, has become immensely popular over the past two years, the technology crash notwithstanding (see chart 5). Many companies and individuals leave their access-points open deliberately to enable passers-by to share their Internet connections. Open a laptop in New York, San Francisco, Seattle or many other large cities around the world and you may well be able to get online free. But although Wi-Fi is liberating for users, it can cause security problems.

B Adding an access-point to a network costs less than $200 and is very simple—so simple, in fact, that 'rogue' access-points have started to sprout on corporate networks without the knowledge of management. A survey by *Computerworld*, an industry magazine, found that 30% of American companies had identified rogue access-points on their networks. And

[1] Wi-Fi is short for 'Wireless Fidelity', the brand name of the original license for computer wireless network technology.

if these are left open, they provide a back door past the firewall into the company's network. Rob Clyde, chief technology officer at Symantec, says that half of the chief executives at a recent round-table event cited Wi-Fi as a top security concern.

This is just one example of how a new technology can bring security problems in its wake. There are plenty of others. Some firms are opening up their networks through online business-to-business exchanges, for example, where they list what they want to buy or sell and invite bids. Everything from paper clips to car components is bought or sold in this way. There is widespread agreement that 'web services', in which companies open up their core business processes directly to other firms over the Internet, will become increasingly important in the next few years. But by opening its systems to outsiders, a company may also attract unwanted visitors, or attacks from nosy competitors.

C Joint ventures, in which two firms collaborate and share information, can also cause problems. A recent report by Vista Research cites the example of an American car maker that established a joint venture with a Japanese firm and opened up its network to allow in employees of its Japanese partner. But the design of the American firm's network allowed access only on an 'all or nothing' basis, so the Japanese firm's employees ended up with access to everything.

Hand-held computers are another problem. They are often used to store sensitive data such as passwords, bank details and calendars. 'The calendar is a fundamental loophole,' says Doug Dedo of Microsoft's mobile devices division, because it may contain entries such as 'meeting with company X re merger'. Another problem associated with hand-held computers is that their users carry them into the office and plug them into their computers, bypassing anti-virus systems and firewalls. A virus-infected document stored on a hand-held computer could then start spreading. Similarly, peer-to-peer file-swapping networks such as Gnutella, instant-messaging services that zap messages and files across the Internet, and web-based e-mail systems such as Hotmail all provide new routes into a company's network that can be exploited by attackers.

D There are plenty of technical fixes available. Hand-held scanners can be used to track down rogue access-points, and legitimate access-points can be secured against outsiders by using virtual-private-network (VPN) software. A lot of work is being done to ensure that web services are secure, including, improbably, a joint initiative by rivals Microsoft and IBM. Anti-virus and firewall software exists for hand-held computers, which can also be password-protected. And firewalls can be configured to prevent unauthorised use of peer-to-peer and instant-messaging services.

E All these threats arise from a common factor: the distinction between the 'public' parts of a company's network (such as the web servers where its home page resides) and the private core (which is accessible only to employees) is quickly eroding. 'The cultural and technological trend is towards more porous companies,' says Gene Hodges, president of Network Associates, a large security-software firm. As firms connect with their suppliers and customers, 'the more you open up, the more you are exposed.'

F The classic notion of perimeter security, in short, is fast becoming obsolete. Alan Henricks, chief executive of Cenzic, says the shift is 'from keeping people out to bringing people in in a trusted fashion'. Nand Mulchandani, co-founder of Oblix, another security firm, puts it more colourfully: the 'big walls, moat and crocodiles' approach of the past few years, he says, is now outdated.

The latest thinking is that rather than seeing their networks as castles, large organisations should regard them as airports. People go in and out all the time, some areas are more secure than others, and as people pass from one area to another they have to present their credentials: tickets, boarding passes or passports. Apply this approach to computer security, and instead of an 'exclusive' model in which you try to prevent people from doing things they shouldn't, you have an 'inclusive' model that lays down who can do what, and only lets certain people do certain things.

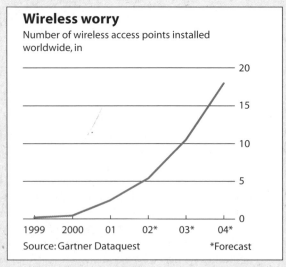

Wireless worry
Number of wireless access points installed worldwide, in

Source: Gartner Dataquest   *Forecast

Question 7

Choose the most appropriate title for Reading Passage 8 from the list below.

List of titles
A Computer networks and company credentials
B Wireless networks and security
C Secure passwords
D The future of online commerce

Questions 8–11

Do the following statements agree with the views of the writer in Reading Passage 8?

Write:

YES   if the statement agrees with the views of the writer
NO   if the statement disagrees with the views of the writer
NOT GIVEN   if it is not possible to say what the writer thinks about this

8   Access-points can make networks vulnerable to unwelcome intrusions.
9   It is surprising that Microsoft and IBM should be working together.
10 It is quite difficult to install an illegal access-point to a company network.
11 The latest firewalls should be included in all network designs.

Questions 12–13

Answer the questions below. Choose **NO MORE THAN THREE WORDS** from Reading Passage 8 for each answer.

12 According to the new model of network security, what will users have to do to pass from one area to another? ....

13 Who is authorized to access the private area of a company network?

....

Questions 14–17

Match the opinions **14–17** with the person who holds the opinion. Write the correct letter **A–E** by the sentences **14–17** below.

NB You may use any letter more than once.

14 Companies are becoming more transparent.
15 Wireless access is a security issue.
16 The diary function on a computer is a vulnerable area for a system.
17 The policy of excluding the public from networks is old-fashioned.

Opinion held by:

A Rob Clyde
B Doug Dedo
C Gene Hodges
D Alan Henricks
E Nand Mulchandani

Questions 18–20

Look at the chart from Reading Passage 8 and answer the following questions.

18 In what year was wireless access first installed? ....
19 How many access points were expected to be installed in 2002? ....
20 In what year was the installation of wireless access points expected to double that of 2002? ....

Check your answers on page 103.

Study Skills: Writing

How much do you know about the IELTS Academic Writing module?
Do the quiz below to find out.

Quiz

1 How long is the writing paper?
  A 40 minutes
  B 60 minutes
  C 90 minutes

2 How long should you spend on each task?
  A 20 minutes for Task 1 and 40 minutes for Task 2
  B 30 minutes for Task 1 and 60 minutes for Task 2

3 Is it a good idea to take longer than this for Task 1? Why?
  A Yes
  B No

4 How much do you have to write for each task?
  A Minimum 150 words for Task 1 and 250 words for Task 2
  B Minimum 250 words for Task 1 and 350 words for Task 2

5 What kind of writing do you have to do for Task 1?
  A Describing a diagram
  B Writing a diary entry
  C Writing a formal letter

6 What kind of writing do you have to do for Task 2?
  A A report on a book you have read
  B An essay discussing an issue of general interest
  C An article for a newspaper

Writing Task 1

Skills development

Understanding the task

The instructions

In Task 1 you have to look at information from a chart, table, diagram or graph and present it in the form of a text. The instruction tells you to 'Summarize the information by selecting and reporting the main features and make comparisons where relevant.'

Task types

Look at figures **1–6** and decide which ones are about:

1 Change over time
2 Proportions (check this word if you don't know it)
3 A process

Figure 1. Production of Sugar

```
[Sugar beet crop grows] → [Harvesting] → [Chopping & cleaning] → [Boiling]
                                                                      ↓
                                                                    Juice
                                                                      ↓
                                                                 [Filtering]
                                                                      ↓
                                                                  Crystals
                                                                      ↓
[Packing] ← Granules ← [Granulation process] ← White sugar ← [Centrifuge]
```

Figure 2. Life expectancy in the UK

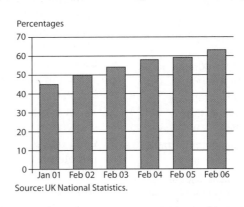

Females

Males

Projections

Source: UK National Statistics.

Figure 3. Percentage of the population in six countries who can speak a second language

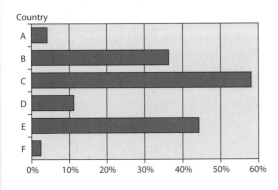

Country

A, B, C, D, E, F

0% 10% 20% 30% 40% 50% 60%

Figure 4. Attendance at cultural events in Great Britain

						Percentages
	1986/87	1991/92	1996/97	1999/00	2000/01	2001/02
Cinema	31	44	54	56	55	57
Plays	23	23	24	23	23	24
Art	21	21	22	22	21	22
Classical	12	12	12	12	12	12
Ballet	6	6	7	6	6	6
Opera	5	6	7	6	6	6
Contemporary	4	3	4	4	4	5
Percentage of resident population aged 15 and over						

Source: UK National Statistics.

Figure 5. Numbers of various types of restaurants in the city of Gastronome

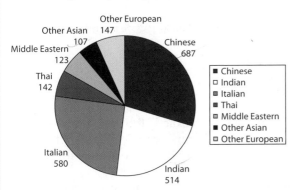

Other European 147
Other Asian 107
Middle Eastern 123
Thai 142
Italian 580
Indian 514
Chinese 687

- Chinese
- Indian
- Italian
- Thai
- Middle Eastern
- Other Asian
- Other European

Figure 6. Adults accessing the internet in the UK

Percentages

70, 60, 50, 40, 30, 20, 10, 0

Jan 01 Feb 02 Feb 03 Feb 04 Feb 05 Feb 06

Source: UK National Statistics.

Talking about the chart

1 Which figure **1–6** tells you:

1 what proportion of British adults used the internet in 2004?
2 how many people go to see plays at the theatre?
3 how long men and women lived, on average, in 1981?
4 the percentage of people in Country E who can speak two languages?
5 the number of Chinese restaurants in Gastronome?
6 about sugar production?

2 Which of the figures **1–6** can you also refer to as:

a chart?
a diagram?
a pie chart?
a flow chart?
a table?
a bar chart?
a graph?
a line graph?

3 Can you identify the following in figures **1–6**? Where?

a segment
a category
a stage
an axis (*plural*: axes /ˈæksiːz/)
a step
a column
a row
a projection

Reading the chart

Look at figures **1–6** and find this information.

1 What happens to the juice after the boiling stage?
2 How long, on average, did men and women live in 1961?
3 What percentage of people in Country B speak a second language?
4 Which country has the largest percentage of second language speakers? What was the exact figure?
5 Give a fraction which means almost the same as 31% (eg 26% is just over a quarter).
6 Which three types of food account for more than three-quarters of the restaurants in Gastronome?
7 What was the most popular sort of cultural event in Britain in each of the years shown?
8 Only one sort of cultural event was popular with exactly the same number of people every year. Which? What proportion of British people attended it?
9 What was the least popular sort of cultural event in Britain in each of the years shown?
10 Which country has the smallest proportion of second language speakers?
11 What percentage of British adults used the internet in February 2005?
12 What is the result of the filtering process?

Remember
- You have to summarize the information
  - by selecting and reporting the main features
  - and make comparisons where relevant.
- So your first step is to understand the information.
- If you are not comfortable with diagrams, you need plenty of practice. Study charts like Figures 1–6 in newspapers and magazines each week. Spend a few minutes understanding each one.
- If you do this regularly, it will get much easier – and quicker.

Selecting the main features

1 Look at Figure 2 and answer the questions. Then check your ideas on page 104.

1 What is the diagram about?
2 What are the main features?
3 What exceptions can you see to any trends?
4 What comparisons are relevant?

2 Now look at Figure 6 and answer the questions above. Then check your ideas on page 104.

Writing an introduction

Introductions 1: The topic

1 Read the sample question and possible introduction for your answer below. How has the introduction been reworded?

The graph shows life expectancy for males and females in the UK from 1901 to 2025.

Possible introduction for your answer:

The line graph gives average lengths of life for men and women in the UK between 1901 and 2025. The figures from about 2002 onwards are projections.

2 For each question below, write a possible introduction.

1 Question: The chart shows the incidence of low birthweight in a number of regions of the world.

....

2 Question: The table shows percentage attendance figures for seven types of cultural event in Great Britain between 1986–7 and 2001–2.

....

3 Question: The chart shows the number of underweight children aged 5 or below in seven regions of the world.

....

4 Question: The chart shows UK citizens' spending on three types of reading materials.

....

5 Question: The chart illustrates the world's mobile phone subscribers in 2006, showing their distribution between six geographical regions.

....

6 Question: The chart gives information about the activities on weekdays of adults in the UK aged 16 and over at various times throughout the 24-hour cycle.

....

7 Question: The table and chart show regional and global population changes between 1950 and 2000 as well as the increase in urban populations in the same period, with a projection for 2050.

....

8 Question: The chart shows the percentage change in serious crimes recorded by the police in European Union countries between 1996 and 2000.

....

> **Remember**
> Tell the reader what the diagram is about but you mustn't repeat the question. You need to be able to re-word the question quickly. This takes some practice. Don't worry if it's hard at first – keep practising.

> **Remember**
> ... *between* 1901 *and* 2025
> ... *from* 1901 *to* 2025
> ... *starting in* 1901 *and ending in* 2025
> ... *for a* 5-*year period beginning in* 2000

> **Tip**
> Check your answers one by one on page 105. Don't do them all before checking – you'll learn more by checking each one in turn.

9   Question: The flow chart shows the chocolate production process.

....

....

3 Read the questions above again and the sample answers on page 105 and <u>underline</u> any phrases that you would like to remember.

Introductions 2: An overview

<table>
<tr><td valign="top">

Remember
- You have to summarize the data in order to get a good mark for Task Achievement.
- A good way to start is by putting an overall comment in the introduction.

</td><td valign="top">

Exam information
There are four criteria for which you get marks. These are:
- Task Achievement (how well you do the task)
- Coherence and Cohesion (organization and linking of ideas and sentences)
- Lexical Resource (vocabulary)
- Grammatical Range and Accuracy

The four criteria are equally important.

</td></tr>
</table>

Look at Figure 2, the notes you made about the main features of the data (page 51) and the comments (page 51). What single, overall comment could you make about the information?

Here is a suggested answer.

They show a massive increase in life expectancy for both women and men – and that women tend to live longer.

Now experiment with writing similar sentences for Figures 3–6.

1   Figure 3

....

2   Figure 4

....

3   Figure 5

....

4   Figure 6

....

Introductions 3: Putting it together

We now have this introductory paragraph for Figure 2:

The line graph gives average lengths of life for men and women in the UK between 1901 and 2025. The figures from about 2002 onwards are projections. They show a massive increase in life expectancy for both women and men – and that women tend to live longer.

Assemble the work you have done, and the suggestions above, to make introductory paragraphs for Figures 3–6.

Skills development: Tasks focusing on proportion

Language focus: Comparisons and numbers

1 Complete the sentences with *as, more, less, that* or *than*.

1   More people go fishing .... play football.
2   It's not .... interesting .... the other one.
3   This is .... interesting .... that.
4   You're right. It's .... interesting than the other.
5   But it's not .... useful.
6   China is bigger .... India.
7   London is .... polluted than Oslo.

2 Look at the table and complete the sentences below. Use the words in the box. You can use the same phrase more than once.

Estimated population	
Canada	33 098 932
Russia	142 893 540
Oman	3 102 229
Germany	82 422 299
Belize	287 730
Japan	127 463 611
Liberia	3 042 004

1 Russia has .... population.
2 .... more people in Russia than Oman.
3 Germany has a .... population than Canada.
4 Liberia has a .... population than Oman.
5 Liberia's population is almost .... Oman's.
6 Canada's population is about ten times .... of Oman's.
7 Canada's population is about ten times .... as Oman's.
8 Russia's population is about .... as big as Germany's.
9 Russia's population is about .... the size of Germany's.

the size	as big
(slightly) smaller	twice
there are	the biggest
(much) bigger	the same as

Now check your answers on page 105.

Language focus: Proportions

There are two main ways of talking about proportions: by using *percentages* and *fractions*. Here are some ways to use them in sentences.

Well over
More than
Just over
	a quarter
	a third
	two-thirds
	three-quarters
		of	the income is from agriculture.
			the money was spent on
			   books.
			the people questioned said …
			farmers are losing money.
			the damage was caused by
			   fire.
			marriages end in divorce.
			the coffee harvest is exported.

About Roughly Approximately	half all		
Almost Just under Less than Well under	1% 25% 25.3%		
	The majority A minority Most Not much/many Very little/few	of	

1 Complete the sentences about the following table.

You should spend about 20 minutes on this task.

The table below shows attendance at various categories of cultural event in Britain from 1986–7 to 2001–2.

Summarize the information by selecting and reporting the main features and make comparisons where relevant.

Write at least 150 words.

Attendance at Cultural Events in Britain from 1986–7 to 2001–2

						Percentages
	1986/87	1991/92	1996/97	1999/00	2000/01	2001/02
Cinema	31	44	54	56	55	57
Plays	23	23	24	23	23	24
Art galleries/exhibitions	21	21	22	22	21	22
Classical music	12	12	12	12	12	12
Ballet	6	6	7	6	6	6
Opera	5	6	7	6	6	6
Contemporary dance	4	3	4	4	4	5

Note: Figures show percentages of people who said they attend at least once a month.

Source: UK National Statistics.

1 More people went to the cinema in 2001–2 .... in 1986–7.
2 Cinema was .... as popular in 2001–2 as in 1986–7.
3 Cinema was .... popular as theatre from 1996–7 onwards.
4 .... the people sampled went to the cinema in 2001–2.
5 Cinema was over .... popular as contemporary dance in 2001–2.
6 .... a quarter of the people sampled went to the theatre in 2001–2.
7 Cinema was .... popular type of event.
8 Theatre was .... popular type of event.
9 Contemporary dance was .... popular type of event.

2 Now make similar sentences about the table below.

Estimated population	
France	60 876 136
Italy	58 133 509
South Africa	44 187 637
Sudan	41 236 378
Australia	20 264 082
New Zealand	4 076 140

Planning your answer

Step 1 – Analyse the data

- Make notes on the Question Paper. You can use circles and arrows and <u>underline</u> whatever you like.
- Remember you need to summarize the information and make comparisons where relevant.

- So mark any points that you think it's necessary to include – the main points. You don't need to include all the details.
- Also notice, and mark, any comparisons which need making.

Step 2 – Organize your material

- Decide a logical order for your points.
- Decide what to include in your overview in the introductory paragraph. Make sure the overview is strong.
- Make sure you know how many paragraphs you are writing and what points to include in each.
- Think about how you will be able to link the paragraphs as you write.

Checklist for a good answer
Introduction
Does it say what the data is about? ❑
Does it avoid repeating the words used in the question? ❑
Does it give a strong, effective overview? ❑
Plan
Is there a logical order of paragraphs? ❑
Paragraphs
Does each paragraph have a clear point or set of points? ❑
Is the subject of the paragraph clear to the reader? ❑
Do sentences follow on logically from each other? ❑
Does the writer use language well to link sentences together? ❑
Length
Is it long enough? ❑

---

1 Analyse the table about attendance at cultural events on page 54. Use the notes in Step 1, above, to help you.

2 Decide how to organize your material into an answer. Use the notes in Step 2, above, to help you.

3 Read the sample answer below. Use the checklist above to help you decide if it is a good answer.

The table illustrates the percentages of British people who went at least once a month to seven types of cultural event in six 12-month periods, beginning in 1986–7 and ending in 2001–2. Over those 15 years, cinema's position as the most popular type of event strengthened enormously, while there was little or no change in any other category.

Looking first at cinema attendance, this grew by 13% from 1986–7 to 1991–2 and another 10% in the following five years. It continued to rise between 1996–7 and 2000–2, although more slowly and with fluctuations, to finish at 57% in 2001–2. Overall, then, British people's cinema attendance rose by 26% over the 15 years.

This makes a strange comparison with the figures for the other types of event, none of which varied by more than 1–2% over the whole period. The categories were: plays (24% in 2001–2), art galleries/exhibitions (22%), classical music (12%), ballet (6%), opera (6%) and contemporary dance (5%). Classical music was the only category showing no change at all in the years for which data is shown.

Check your ideas about questions 1–3 above on page 106.

Skills practice

Remember

- Select the main features.
  Make sure you do not
  simply write a list of all the
  information. Make sure
  the main points stand out.
- This probably means not
  reporting all the figures
  (although in this case
  there are very few so you
  probably will report most
  or all).
- Remember what you have
  learned about writing an
  introduction.
- You must write at least 150
  words. In the exam you
  will have only 20 minutes,
  so don't allow yourself to
  write too much when you
  practise. 190 words is a
  sensible maximum.
- Count the words you have
  written (each word, not
  just an estimate). This
  is good training for the
  exam, when you will not
  have time – but will need
  to know how much you
  have written without
  counting.

Study the chart below. Remember that you have to <u>summarize the information</u> by <u>selecting and reporting the main features</u> and <u>make comparisons</u> where relevant.

1. Make notes about the main features and decide what comparisons to make.
2. Make a brief plan.
3. Write an answer to the question.

Writing Task 1

You should spend about 20 minutes on this task.

The chart below shows the proportions of graduates from Bluesky University in 2006 entering different employment sectors.

Summarize the information by selecting and reporting the main features, and make comparisons where relevant.

Write at least 150 words.

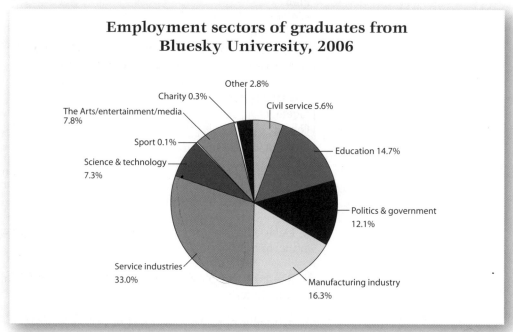

Employment sectors of graduates from Bluesky University, 2006

Other 2.8%
Charity 0.3%
Civil service 5.6%
The Arts/entertainment/media 7.8%
Sport 0.1%
Education 14.7%
Science & technology 7.3%
Politics & government 12.1%
Service industries 33.0%
Manufacturing industry 16.3%

Now look at the sample answer on page 106.

Skills development: Tasks focusing on *change over time*

Here is an example of a *Change over time* question.

You should spend about 20 minutes on this task.

The graph below illustrates the number of visits made to and from the UK between 1984 and 2004.

Summarize the information by selecting and reporting the main features, and make comparisons where relevant.

Write at least 150 words.

Study Skills: Writing

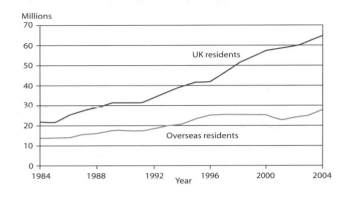

International travel to and from the UK

Source: UK National Statistics.

Proportional change

1 Look at the numbers of UK residents making trips abroad and overseas residents visiting the UK. Compare the figures for 1984 with those for 2004.

1 Which one doubled?
2 Which one tripled?

2 Use the two-step approach to planning on pages 54–55 to study the diagram and make a plan. Remember to work through the *Checklist for a good answer* on page 55.

Check your ideas by looking at the sample answer on page 106.

3 People really do write texts like the ones you are practising. This is what the UK government says about the subject of the chart. The text is twice the length you'll write in Task 1, but it uses some good language for IELTS Task 1. It also has more information than you can see in the chart.

Underline, or use a highlighter to mark, the information which is <u>not</u> shown in the chart.

In 2004 overseas residents made a record 27.8 million visits to the UK and spent a record £13 billion. Taking inflation into account spending by overseas residents increased by 13 per cent between 1984 and 2004, and 7 per cent between 2003 and 2004.

The number of visits to the UK doubled between 1984 and 2004, with levels exceeding the previous high in 1998. Between 2003 and 2004 there was a 16 per cent increase in the number of holiday visits to the UK by overseas residents. This followed a decline of 18 per cent between 2000 and 2001, and only small recoveries in each of the following two years.

Residents of the USA made the largest number of visits to the UK – 3.6 million in 2004. French residents made 3.3 million visits, followed by residents of Germany (3.0 million visits), Ireland (2.6 million) and the Netherlands (1.6 million).

The number of visits abroad made by UK residents has almost tripled since 1984, to a record 64.2 million visits in 2004. Two-thirds of these visits abroad were holidays, just under half of which were package holidays. Although the number of holidays overall has continued to increase year-on-year, there has been little change in the number of package holidays in the last five years.

Europe remained the most popular destination for UK residents, accounting for over 80 per cent of visits abroad. Spain continued to be the most popular country to visit, with 13.8 million visits in 2004. France was second in popularity, with 11.6 million visits. The number of visits by UK residents to the USA increased by 15 per cent in 2004 to 4.2 million, although this was still 4 per cent lower than the number in 2000.

Spending on visits abroad by UK residents increased to a record £30.3 billion, a fourfold increase between 1984 and 2004 in real terms, and a 10 per cent increase between 2003 and 2004.

Check your answers on page 106.

4 Look again at the whole text. Underline any phrases you think are useful for describing information. Compare your answers with the notes on page 107.

Verbs and nouns of change

1 Use the words in the box below to label the diagrams.

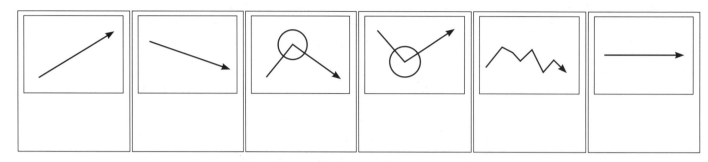

drop	fall
bottom out	peak
be unchanged	stay the same
rise	go up
fluctuate	

2 Fill in the table with the missing form. A shaded box means there is no noun form.

Note
Some of these verbs have no exact noun form but there are others we can use:
- *go up* – *a rise* or *an increase*
- *bottom out* – *a low point*
- *be unchanged* or *stay the same* – *a steady period* or *a plateau.*

Verb	Noun
rise	a rise
go up	███████
increase	
fall	
drop	
decrease	
peak	
bottom out	███████
fluctuate	
be unchanged	███████
stay the same	███████

Remember
- *to rise gradually* but *a gradual rise*
- *... rose from 70 to 90 = rose by 20* (verb + *by*)
- *a rise from 70 to 90 = a rise of 20* (noun + *of*)
- Sales stood *at* £1 million.
- There was a rise/fall *in* sales.

3 Look at the graph on page 59 relating to measles, mumps and rubella and complete the following sentences.

1 Measles cases .... rapidly in 1993.
2 There was a rise .... about 11,000 measles cases in 1993.
3 In 1991, mumps infections stood .... about 4,000.
4 Rubella cases .... in 1996.
5 There was a dramatic fall .... measles cases between 1994 and 2001.
6 Mumps cases went up .... more than 15,000 in 2003.
7 There was an increase .... more than 15,000 mumps cases in 2003.

Expressing contrast

Use language for expressing contrast from the box on the left to write practice sentences about the data from the graphs on page 61.

1 ....
2 ....
3 ....
4 ....

Compare your sentences with the sample answers on page 107.

Planning your answer

Look again at the two-step guide to planning on page 54. Then study the task below.

1 Step 1: Analyse the data. Remember to make notes on the chart itself, using circles, arrows, etc. Check your work by looking at the notes on page 107.

You should spend about 20 minutes on this task.

The chart (below) shows the numbers of new cases of three infectious diseases in the UK between 1991 and 2004.

Summarize the information by selecting and reporting the main features, and make comparisons where relevant.

Write at least 150 words.

> **Note**
> *Although* + *noun* + *verb*
> Although prices rose, sales increased.
> Sales increased, although prices rose.
> *Despite* + *noun*
> Despite price reductions, sales fell.
> Sales rose despite price increases.
> *In spite of* + *noun*
> In spite of price reductions, sales fell.
> Sales rose in spite of price increases.
> *Statement* + *In contrast* + *noun* + *verb*
> Rainfall decreased. In contrast, temperatures rose.

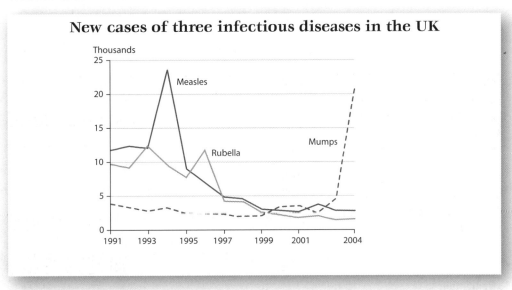

New cases of three infectious diseases in the UK

Source: UK National Statistics.

2 Step 2: Organize your material

1 Look at the following three approaches. Which do you think is best?
  Approach 1: Say what happened in each year from 1991 to 2004.
  Approach 2: Talk about each disease separately.
  Approach 3: Talk about the main features you identified.

2 Think about paragraphing. First, think about the following points. Use the checklist on page 55 to help you.

> **Introduction**
> Say what the data is about. ❑
> Give a strong, effective overview. ❑
> **Plan for paragraphs**
> Decide logical order of paragraphs. ❑
> Give each paragraph a clear point or set of points. ❑

3   Then think about these points.

> **Introduction**
> Avoid repeating the words used in the question.   ❏
> **Paragraphs**
> Make the subject of each paragraph clear to the reader.   ❏
> Make sure your sentences follow on from each other in a
> logical order.   ❏
> Try to link sentences together.   ❏
> **Length**
> Make sure your answer is long enough.   ❏

3 Writing up your answer

You are now ready to write up your answer, although in this case one has been prepared for you.

Read the following sample answer.

1   Mark it, following the checklist above.
2   In particular look at the way the writer uses language to link paragraphs and sentences, to make clear the relationships between ideas and information. Underline any language of this kind.

> The graph gives approximate figures for UK measles, mumps and rubella infections between 1991 and 2004. Despite large variations, it shows a general fall until a sudden increase in mumps in the last two years.
>
> Cases of measles and rubella tended to fall, although there were sudden rises in both, causing peaks of 23 000 for measles in 1994 and 12 000 for rubella two years later. Both then showed remarkable falls and followed very similar trends from 1997 to 2004, with the rate of measles infections being generally a little higher.
>
> In contrast, mumps cases fluctuated between 2 000 and 4 000 until 1999 and, although they began to rise a little, all three diseases had very low rates (below 4 000) until 2002.
>
> At this point the figures for mumps began to rise, first rapidly and then more so, to reach 21 000 in 2004, with no indication of a slowdown – compared with a level of 4 000 in 1991. The corresponding figures for measles were a fall from 12 000 cases in 1991 to 3 000 in 2004; and for rubella, from 10 000 to 2 000.   (179 words)

Combined tasks

Study the task below. Use the instructions above to make notes for an answer. Check your ideas by looking at the sample answer on page 108.

You should spend about 20 minutes on this task.

The graphs below show the percentage of adults accessing the internet in the United Kingdom between January 2001 and February 2006, and the percentage of households with various kinds of internet connections during part of the same period.

Summarize the information by selecting and reporting the main features and make comparisons where relevant.

Write at least 150 words.

> **Remember**
> Task 1 questions sometimes combine two data sources. You could get a graph and table together, for example. Their content will be related. With combined questions follow the two-step planning process as usual and:
> - make an overall comment in your introduction which summarizes both;
> - be sure to summarize both sources by reporting the main features of both. Make comparisons within and between both sources if relevant.

Adults accessing the internet in the UK

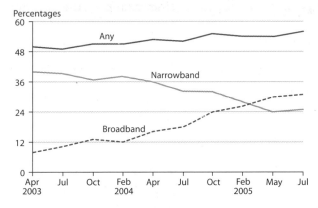

Household internet connections

Source: *UK National Statistics.*

Skills practice

Study the task below.

1 Make notes about the main features and decide what comparisons to make.
2 Make a brief plan.
3 Write an answer to the question. Then read the sample answer on page 108.

You should spend about 20 minutes on this task.

The graph shows the percentages of male and female populations in the United Kingdom who smoked in the years from 1974 to 2004–5.

Summarize the information by selecting and reporting the main features and make comparisons where relevant.

Write at least 150 words.

Percentages of the male and female populations who smoke

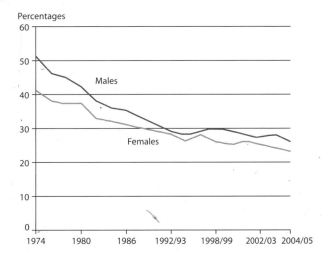

Source: *UK National Statistics.*

Skills development: Tasks focusing on processes

Remember
You have to describe the main features of the data. This means the stages and whatever the diagram explains about the processes. But you do not need to add your own information: your job is to report what the diagram shows.

Remember
Most of the planning is done for you:
You write about the steps in the process, which are shown on the diagram. You will probably not need (or be able) to make many comparisons.

Understanding the question

Step 1   Read the task first. Notice that it explains the subject of the diagram. Look quickly at the whole diagram, the title and the main stages.

Step 2   Decide if it is a cyclical process, or one which has a start and end.

Step 3   Look at what the diagram tells you about each stage.

Planning your answer

Step 1   Decide on a logical starting point:

- If the process has a start and end, as in Figure 1 on page 49, then the starting point is obvious (eg the crop growing in Figure 1).

- If the process is cyclical, identify a logical place to start your description.

Step 2   Follow the two-step planning process:

- Introduction: Explain what the diagram shows. If possible, make an overall comment about the end result or the process itself.
- Describe each stage in turn.

Now look at the question below. Make a plan for answering it before looking at the sample answer on page 109.

You should spend about 20 minutes on this task.

The diagram shows the process by which glass drinks bottles are recycled.

Summarize the information by selecting and reporting the main features and make comparisons where relevant.

Write at least 150 words.

Glass drinks bottle recycling process

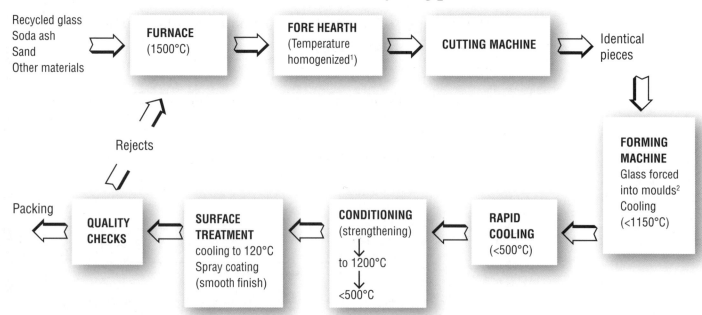

[1] Homogenized means 'made the same'.
[2] A mould is 'a shaped container into which you pour a liquid that then becomes solid in the shape of the container'. (*Macmillan English Dictionary*)

Writing your answer

Active or passive?

1 Look at the sample answer on page 109 about recycling glass bottles. <u>Underline</u> each passive verb and notice the active verbs too. Check your answers on page 109. Think about how you could use the same language in your answer.

2 Decide which version of each sentence is better. Remember, sometimes both forms (active or passive) are acceptable.

1 A The liquids are mixed in a mixing chamber.
   B People mix the liquids in a mixing chamber.

2 A The director chooses his team.
   B A team is chosen.

3 A Technicians heat the water.
   B The water is heated.

4 A The mixture is boiled.
   B We boil the mixture.

5 A The gas passes along the pipe.
   B The gas is passed along the pipe.

6 A The mixture passes through a filter.
   B The mixture is filtered.

7 A The mixture is filtered through a filter.
   B The mixture passes through a filter, which removes impurities.

8 A People test the product.
   B The product is tested.
   C The product undergoes testing.

9 A Scanners irradiate the product to kill germs.
   B The product is irradiated to kill germs.
   C The product undergoes irradiation to kill germs.

Now check your answers on page 109.

Describing stages

Study the task below and complete the sentences using the language in the tables to help you. Notice how passive and active forms are mixed. The passive forms of verbs are shown in italics.

You should spend about 20 minutes on this task.

The diagram shows the process by which salt is removed from sea water to produce fresh water.

Summarize the information by selecting and reporting the main features and make comparisons where relevant.

Write at least 150 words.

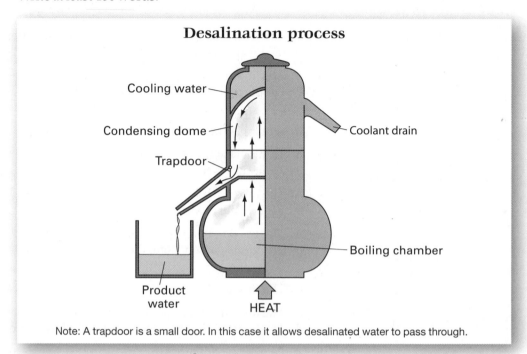

Desalination process

Cooling water

Condensing dome

Trapdoor

Coolant drain

Boiling chamber

Product water

HEAT

Note: A trapdoor is a small door. In this case it allows desalinated water to pass through.

(1) ...., salt water *is heated* in a boiling chamber. From (2) .... it passes
(3) .... a membrane (4) .... the condensing dome, (5) .... it *is cooled*.
(6) .... it passes through a trapdoor and (7) .... the 'product water' container.

In (8) .... the cooling water *is provided* by a separate system. When it *has been heated* by the water in the condensing dome, it flows away (9) .... a coolant drain.

Steps and sequencing		
The first The second The next A further The final	stage step	is ...
First Next Then After that		
... and the cycle / process begins again.		

Routes					
From here it	passes travels moves	(along (through (via	a pipe)	to	a chamber
From here there are two possible routes ...					
If the sample is approved, then it moves on to ... If the sample fails the test, then it ...					

Saying what happens at each stage				
... into ... to	a	container chamber mixing chamber	where (things happen) in which (things happen) during which (things happen)	
			which (does things)	
The next stage is	finishing cleaning	which	involves includes	washing, brushing and polishing. three main elements:

Writing Task 2

Quiz

Answer true or false

1 You should take 40 minutes for Task 2.

2 You can choose to take 35 or 30 minutes for Task 2.

3 You need to write 300 words.

4 It is important to give reasons for your answer.

5 You should read the whole question before you start writing.

6 If the question topic is familiar, you can start writing at once.

7 There are extra marks for writing very long answers.

8 You should write your Task 2 answer first and do Task 1 second.

Skills development 1: Organizing your answer

Understanding the task

Look at questions **1–6** below and decide which question type A, B or C each task is.

Type A	Type B	Type C
You need to explain your views and come to a conclusion. (You do not need to write about other people's viewpoints or ideas, but you must show how your ideas and views support your conclusion.)	You need to look at different viewpoints as well as your own and come to a conclusion. (You need to say where you think the balance is between differing points of view. It is not enough simply to say that people disagree.)	You need to list some causes of a problem and suggest some possible solutions. (You need to show how the factors you list cause the problem; and how the solutions you suggest would help.)

Exam tip

In the exam you need to decide quickly which type of question you are dealing with but the wording is not always the same.

Questions

1

Millions of people in the world do not have enough to eat.

What do you think are some of the causes of this problem and what measures could be taken to reduce it?

Question type ☐

2

People who commit serious crimes should be kept in prison for as long as possible to ensure that they cannot commit more crimes.

Do you agree or disagree?

Question type ☐

3

Many people argue that exams are the best way to assess people's competence and that no better system has yet been found. Others say they are unfair, unhelpful and out of date.

Do you think the benefits of exams outweigh the disadvantages?

Question type ☐

4

Choose three of the following media and say how effective you think they are as sources of news. Which do you think is the most effective?

- Radio
- TV
- Magazines
- The internet
- Newspapers

Question type ☐

5

Money is important in most people's lives, although some people think it is more important than others.

What do you feel are the right uses of money? What other factors are important for a good life?

Question type ☐

6

Some people feel the private lives of politicians, film stars, sports personalities and other well-known people should remain private; others say there are good reasons why they should not.

Discuss both these views and give your own opinion.

Question type ☐

Now check your answers on page 110.

Preparing your answer

General approach

> **Key principles**
> You must:
> - give reasons for your answer.
> - support your arguments with examples and relevant evidence.
> You are writing for a general, non-specialist reader. You can use you own ideas, knowledge and experience.

Planning

> **Why plan?**
> **Your answer needs:**
> - relevant ideas.
> - clear organization.
> - signposting. Good organization is not enough. You need to make that organization clear to the reader, for example by starting each paragraph by explaining its purpose: 'There are many reasons why famous people should be allowed privacy.'
> *Above all, you need to answer the question directly. The argument should be like an arrow from the first paragraph to the last.*
> **How long?**
> Use 5 minutes for planning, and about 30 minutes for writing. The more you practise planning answers, the easier this gets.

Remember
You need to read the whole question in order to understand it properly.

Planning 1: Brainstorming

1 Look at Question 6 again. What question type is it? Where does it tell you what your answer must talk about?

You should spend about 40 minutes on this task.

Write about the following topic:

Some people feel the private lives of politicians, film stars, sports personalities and other well-known people should remain private; others say there are good reasons why they should not.

Discuss both these views and give your own opinion.

Give reasons for your answer and include any relevant examples from your own knowledge or experience.

Write at least 250 words.

2 Take five minutes to brainstorm ideas for Question 6. Write just one or two words to help you remember each idea, not full sentences.

Reasons for privacy	Reasons against privacy

3 Now analyse and then brainstorm further ideas for Question 2 on page 65.

Agree	Disagree

Planning 2: Selecting ideas and evidence

1 Look again at your ideas for Question 6 above. Which ones do you think are the strongest? Which are the weakest and should not be included? Then do the same with the ideas in the grid above. Which are the weakest ideas? Check your answers on page 110.

2 Repeat the question above for Question 2 on page 65.

3 Look at how this statement is made stronger by the supporting example.

Statement: Prison works by stopping criminals from committing more crimes.
Example: Murderers who commit murder again when released from prison.

Think of some examples for these points.

1 **Statement**: The media chase famous people and take private photos to make money, not for moral reasons.
   Example: Intrusive photographs which show celebrities' intimate or embarrassing moments.

2 **Statement**: Celebrities become successful through publicity. They are successful because their lives are a kind of soap opera.
   Example: ....

3 **Statement:** Poor diet can cause illness.
  Examples: ....

4 Explain your most important statements. Read the example below.

Statement: Providing free health care is expensive.
Explanation: Hospitals, clinics, salaries for medical and administrative staff, equipment, treatments and drugs all have to be paid for.

Write an explaination of the point made in each of these statements.

1 **Statement:** Prison is expensive for the country.
  Explanation: ....
  ....

2 **Statement:** Prison works.
  Explanation: ....
  ....

3 **Statement:** Many prisoners simply want to go back to prison when released because they cannot cope with normal life anymore.
  Explanation: ....
  ....

4 **Statement:** Young people are more likely to be lifelong criminals after prison.
  Explanation: ....
  ....

5 **Statement:** Smoking is expensive.
  Explanation: ....
  ....

Planning 3: Deciding your viewpoint

1 Look again at Question 6 and your ideas on page 67. Then read the sample answer below. Do you think it is a good answer?

There is much debate on this topic, but there is no doubt in my mind that famous people have the right to complete privacy in their private lives. In these days there is too much media intrusion and this makes it impossible for people to carry on their own lives.

There are many examples of this. The most obvious one is that of Princess Diana, who died in 1997 after a high-speed car chase possibly because she was trying to escape from photographers who were determined to get an exclusive picture of her. The reason for this is that photographs of famous people sell newspapers. In other words it is entirely a question of money – of profit for media organizations.

On the other hand, there is sometimes a reason for exposing someone's private life in public. Sometimes we find that a politician, perhaps one of the country's leaders, has done something very bad in his private life which people in the country should know about. For example, perhaps he has lied to his family about something very serious over a long period of time. In this case we must ask how honest he is and whether it is sensible for this man to hold such a responsible job in the country.

In conclusion, politicians should not be allowed to hide behind the right to privacy. The public has a right to know what they have done wrong because it may affect their trustworthiness. However, in other cases media intrusion is a serious problem and should be stopped.

(256 words)

Check your ideas on page 111.

2 Think about Question 6 again. What is your point of view?

3 Now think about Question 2 again. What is your point of view?

4 Choose one of the other questions on pages 65–66. Take five minutes to analyse the question and brainstorm ideas then decide your viewpoint. Remember to keep your notes brief.

Planning 4: Planning your answer

This is a question of organization. Put your ideas in a logical order and use paragraphs to do it. In this way you make the best possible use of your ideas and examples.

1 Look again at Question 1 on page 65. Which of the following six answer plans do you think is best?

(Note: Each numbered point represents a paragraph, eg in ONE there are three paragraphs.)

ONE
1 Causes of problem
2 Possible measures to reduce problem
3 Conclusion – change requires international cooperation

TWO
1 Introduction – malnutrition and starvation
2 Causes of problem
3 Conclusion – change requires international cooperation

THREE
1 Introduction – malnutrition and starvation
2 Causes of problem; possible measures to reduce it
3 Conclusion – change requires international cooperation

FOUR
1 Introduction – malnutrition and starvation
2 Possible measures to reduce problem
3 Conclusion – change requires international cooperation

FIVE
1 Introduction – malnutrition and starvation
2 Possible measures to reduce problem
3 Causes of problem
4 Conclusion – change requires international cooperation

SIX
1 Introduction – malnutrition and starvation
2 Causes of problem
3 Possible measures to reduce problem
4 Conclusion – change requires international cooperation

2 Look again at Question 3 on page 65 and the following list of ideas. Put the ideas into a logical paragraph order 1–5.

- Advantages of exams ☐
- Disadvantages of exams ☐
- This is probably the best balance which can be achieved; and often traditional exams are the only possibility ☐
- Exams are not perfect but are a necessity ☐
- Improvements possible by mixing exams with other systems (eg long-term assessment) ☐

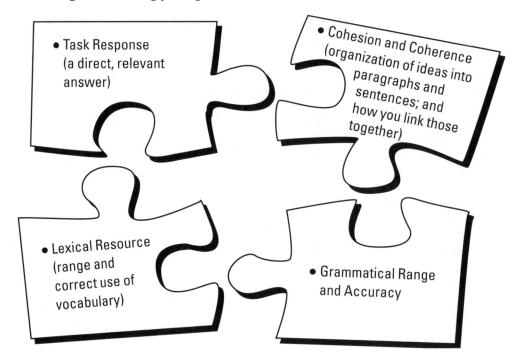

A well-planned answer will score better in the first two categories, *Task response* and *Cohesion & Coherence*.

These **five steps**:

1　brainstorming
2　selecting ideas and evidence
3　deciding your viewpoint
4　planning your answer
5　checking your plan

are a sensible way to make sure you produce the best plan you can.

Here are some statements made by exam candidates. What comments can you make about their approaches?

1　I wrote a really good answer. It's a subject I know lots about and I wrote about 400 words. I don't understand why I didn't get a better result. I'm so disappointed.

2　It was a perfect question for me. I just looked at the topic and started writing straight away – I was so pleased. But they marked me very unfairly and gave me the wrong result.

3　Of course I'm not going to plan – my brain doesn't work that way! I've got lots of good ideas and I know a lot about a lot of things. How hard can it be? You only have to write 250 words.

Skills development 2

Writing your answer

The introduction

Read the introductory paragraphs and comment on their length and the content. Refer to Questions 1, 2 and 3 on page 65 to remind yourself of the questions.

Refer to Questions 1, 2 and 3 on page 65 to remind yourself of the questions.

Remember
- Your introduction should be directly relevant to the question.
- It should point clearly to the main body and the conclusion of your answer.
- You do not need to include much information in the introduction. The information you do include should be directly relevant.
- A good way to make an impression is to include some information that is relevant and will catch the reader's attention. If, for example, you are arguing that the world must organize itself better to fight poverty, you could include the stark fact that almost a billion people in the world are hungry.

Tip
Decide what your conclusion is before you plan your answer. This is the point of view you will be expressing throughout your answer so you need to express it in the introduction as well as in the conclusion.

1

Why do many people in our world not have enough to eat? And how can we change this situation? These are very difficult questions and I do not know the answers. Maybe I think there are too many people.

2

Many people do not like exams and say the examination system is very bad. Other people say exams are good. This is a very hotly debated question, very difficult. And many people disagree. Many experts have written about this subject and there are many discussions and disagreements very often about this topic. Indeed, every coin has two sides. So you can see it is a hard topic.

3

Exams are important events in most people's lives, from childhood through to adulthood. In my own country children begin national exams at the age of 7 and continue until at least 16 – or, for those who go on to university and beyond, exams may continue until they are about 30 years old. This itself demonstrates how much reliance our society places on the system.

4

It is absolutely true that we need to reduce the amount of crime in our society and in order to do that we need to prevent criminals from re-offending. However, prison is not the way to do it.

5

Exams are important events in most people's lives, from childhood through to adulthood. In my own country children begin national exams at the age of 7 and continue until at least 16 – or, for those who go on to university and beyond, exams may continue until they are about 30 years old. This itself demonstrates how much reliance our society places on the system and indeed suggests that it must work; at least reasonably well. On the other hand, it may be that there are other options which could form alternatives to exams, or at least supplement them, in the interests of producing a system which might be less stressful and perhaps more reliable.

Practice

Think again about Question 1 on page 65. Write an introduction saying that the problems include malnutrition and starvation and expressing the view that they can be solved if countries work together. Then compare your introduction with the samples on page 112.

The main body

> **Remember**
> The main body of the essay is like the engine of a car or the processors in a computer: it's the part that does the work. A solid main body explains your viewpoint clearly so the conclusion will seem completely logical.

1 Answer true or false.

1 You should start a new paragraph for each example.
2 You don't really need to plan this part of the essay.
3 The more paragraphs you write, the better.
4 It's a good idea to learn some special phrases you can use to impress the examiner and use them in the first sentence of each paragraph.
5 You should know exactly how many paragraphs you will write, and what you will say in each, before you start the essay.

2 For Question 1 on page 65 we established the following answer plan (page 69):

1 Introduction – malnutrition and starvation
2 Causes of problem
3 Possible measures to reduce problem
4 Conclusion – change requires international cooperation

To plan paragraph 2, put the following ideas into logical groupings.

- Corruption in poor countries: aid goes to the wrong people
- Climate change
- Growing gap between rich and poor
- High population
- Lack of money spent on relief and development
- Unfair trading practices
- Wrong sort of aid

3 Using the ideas from exercise 2 above write down some evidence to support or explain each point you want to make.

> **Remember**
> One of the four criteria the examiners use is *Coherence and Cohesion*. This means the way you link paragraphs, ideas and sentences together.

4 Read and comment on the following paragraph, written from the notes we prepared.

The world's population is very high. Population growth is very high too. The world needs much, much more food. There is a growing gap between rich and poor. Poorer nations are prevented from selling goods at a fair price. There is a lack of aid and it often does not address the underlying problems. Climate change reduces available farming land through expansion of deserts and through flooding.

> **Remember**
> You do not need special language for this. Instead, you need to communicate the overall message of the paragraph clearly.

5 Write an introductory sentence and a concluding sentence for the paragraph above.

Introductory sentence ....

Concluding sentence ....

Language focus: Ordering ideas; linking cause and effect

Look at the language in the box below.

A(n) The One Another	second major final obvious major obvious	problem cause factor priority reason for this example of this measure result of this	is …

(All) (… and)	this	means … causes … results in …

… caused by … … with the result that … … resulting in … … leading to … … which leads to …		
Because … / Because of … / Due to … … because … / … because of … / … due to …		
This (problem) is	made worse compounded exacerbated	by …

Use some of the language in the box to improve the paragraph below.

The world's population is very high. Population growth is very high too. The world needs much, much more food. There is a growing gap between rich and poor. Poorer nations are prevented from selling goods at a fair price. There is a lack of aid and it often does not address the underlying problems. Climate change reduces available farming land through expansion of deserts and through flooding.

Practice

Now plan and write paragraph 3 of Question 1: Possible measures to reduce problem. Remember to write an introductory and concluding sentence. When you have finished, compare your answer with the suggestion on page 113.

The conclusion

1 Answer true or false.

1 You should learn some special phrases to include in the final paragraph.
2 You should include new arguments in the conclusion.
3 If you have written a good introduction and main body, you do not really need a conclusion.
4 You should say the same thing in the conclusion as in the introduction, but in different words.

2 Look at these conclusions for Question 1. What do you think of them?

1 Now you can see what some of the problems are and I have told you how to solve them.
2 Malnutrition and starvation affect millions of human beings. The tragedy of this situation is that it could be solved if the international community were prepared to address it in an organized and determined way.
3 These problems can be solved but only through organized action by the international community.

3 Now write your own conclusion for Question 1. When you have finished, look at the sample answer on page 113.

Skills practice

Cause and effect questions

What are they?

Some task types – where you need to explain your views and come to a conclusion – contain two separate questions and ask you to explain causes and effects. For example:

You should spend about 40 minutes on this task.

Write about the following topic:

Money is important in most people's lives, although some people think it is more important than others.

What do you feel are the right uses of money? What other factors are important for a good life?

Give reasons for your answer and include any relevant examples from your own knowledge or experience.

Write at least 250 words.

How to answer cause and effect questions

1 Follow the five-step approach on page 70.
2 Develop a point of view which includes a response to *both* questions.
3 Address both questions in the main body of your answer. A good way to do this is to write a paragraph about each.

In other words, your approach will be:
Para 1: Introduction (addressing both questions)
Para 2: First question
Para 3: Second question
Para 4: Conclusion (addressing both questions)

---

1 Look at the question about money on page 74. Make notes about your views.

Right uses of money	Other factors important for a good life

Compare your ideas with the notes on page 113.

2 Now look again at both questions:

- What do you feel are the right uses of money?
- What other factors are important for a good life?

Make notes to help you write a conclusion which includes a response to both questions.

Compare your ideas with the notes on page 113.

3 Now use your notes to write an introductory paragraph. When you have done this, read the sample answer on page 113. Remember this is only one point of view and that you could express a very different one, as long as you deal directly with both issues.

Checking your answer

Remember

The examiners look at four aspects of your writing (see page 70, jigsaw diagram). It is important to leave a few moments to check your answer. It is probably too late to make much difference to your scores for Task Response or Coherence and Cohesion, but you may be able to make a difference under Lexical Resource and Grammatical Range and Accuracy.

Remember

These checklists can help you identify some common problems. Try to avoid these problems and check your work in the exam to eliminate them if possible.

1 Read through the lists. Decide which mistakes you are likely to make and tick the box. This will give you a checklist to work from next time you look at one of your own essays, so you can find the mistakes more easily.

Common vocabulary mistakes

- Long words designed to persuade the examiner that your vocabulary is wider than it really is ❏
- Conversational style (eg *really bad, a pity, you know,* etc.) ❏
- Using the same word many times over (try using synonyms instead) ❏
- Clichés (eg *At the end of the day* it is a complex issue) ❏
- Clichés translated from your language (eg *Every coin has two sides.*) ❏
- Slang (eg *cool* or *wicked*) ❏
- Using *And …* or *So…* or *But …* as the first word in a sentence ❏
- *You* in sentences such as *You have to look at both sides of the issue* (Say: *It is important to look at …* or perhaps *We have to …*) ❏

Common grammar mistakes

- Disagreements of number (eg *Many people thinks* or *Lack of resources and time is a problem* or *The country have a solution*) ❏
- Confusing adjectives with adverbs (eg *a really difficulty*) ❏
- Contractions (eg *It's* or *They've*) ❏
- Sentences with no main verb (eg *Like this one.*) ❏
- Complicated sentences where the relationship between the different parts of the sentence is not clear ❏
- Omitting articles (eg _ *Expensive car is _ status symbol in my country.*) ❏
- Unnecessary (ie wrong) articles (eg *The transport is a key issue.*) ❏
- Forgetting relative pronouns (eg *There are many people __ think this [who].*) ❏
- Two subjects in one sentences (eg *There are many people they think this.*) ❏
- Joining two sentences with a comma (eg *There are many aspects to this problem, one of them is money*). Instead, use a full stop or a relative pronoun. (eg *There are many aspects to this problem, one of which is money.*) ❏

Other mistakes

- Single-sentence paragraphs ❏
- Extremely long paragraphs ❏
- Rhetorical questions (asking questions to which you don't expect an answer) It is not always wrong to use these, but generally it is better to tell the reader what you think. ❏

Your own mistakes

Use this space to add any other mistakes which you need to check your writing for.

.... ❏

.... ❏

.... ❏

.... ❏

.... ❏

.... ❏

.... ❏

.... ❏

Spelling mistakes

Use this space to note any words that you often mis-spell.

```
.........................................        .........................................
.........................................        .........................................
.........................................        .........................................
.........................................        .........................................
.........................................        .........................................
.........................................        .........................................
.........................................        .........................................
.........................................        .........................................
.........................................        .........................................
.........................................        .........................................
```

2 Try to find all the mistakes in the following essay. Check your answers on page 114.

A lot of people feels this question have many different answer. Indeed, every coin have two side. In my country there is much debate about this vexed issue and no agreement about the answer.

Some people say exam is good way to find out who is good at a subject and who is not so good. They're right really in one way because if you don't have exams, how can you find out who has learned the necessary skills and information? People often forget that the knowledge is very important, not just skills. There are many people they do not understand this. Exam best way to test how much people know.

But is there a better way? I think nobody have a system can do the job better. Except maybe continuous assessment, when teacher give marks all the year, then at the end of the year they add up all the marks, this gives a score instead of the exam.

In conclusion I can say there are many ways to test what people learn.

Study Skills: Speaking

How much do you know about the IELTS Speaking module?
Do the quiz below to find out.

Quiz

1 What is the Speaking test format?
  A The examiner interviews three candidates together.
  B The examiner interviews two candidates together.
  C The examiner interviews each candidate alone.
  D Candidates interview each other.

2 The Speaking test lasts:
  A 10–15 minutes.
  B 11–14 minutes.
  C 15–20 minutes.
  D 20–30 minutes.

3 How many parts does the Speaking test have?
  A two parts
  B three parts
  C four parts
  D five parts

4 Answer **True/False/Not sure** to the following questions about the different parts of the Speaking test.
  Part 1
  1 This part lasts 3–4 minutes.
  2 You have to give long answers to a small number of questions.
  3 The questions are about familiar topics.
  Part 2
  4 This part lasts 3–4 minutes.
  5 You have to give a speech.
  6 You can prepare what you say before the Speaking test.
  Part 3
  7 This part lasts 4–5 minutes.
  8 You have to give short answers to a large number of questions.
  9 You have to ask the interviewer questions.

Part 1

The topics you need to talk about

All the topics you talk about will be familiar to you and are on everyday subjects.

Which of the following are likely topics for Part 1? Check your ideas by looking at the comments on page 115.

- Your work
- Your country's economic situation
- Your plans for the future
- Films you like
- Your studies
- i-pods
- Your family
- James Bond
- Your home town
- History
- Your country
- Your free time
- The Industrial Revolution
- The price of oil and gas
- Food you like
- Something very sad which has happened in your life

Possible questions

1 Think about the topic 'Your home town'. What questions could the interviewer ask you about this? Make some notes, then look at the ideas on page 115.

2 Now do the same with 'Your work'. Again, check your answers on page 115.

What makes a good answer

You will probably have no difficulty talking about the topics in Part 1 because they're familiar and don't require any special language. The main thing is to answer the question directly.

The best preparation you can do for Part 1 is to get used to answering questions like this.

1 Look at these questions and answers from Part 1. Which answers do you think are good? Check your ideas by looking at the comments on page 115.

A **Examiner:** Do you come from a town, village or city?
Candidate: I come from Cadiz. It's the capital of Cadiz Province in Andalusia in the south of Spain. Cadiz is a medium-sized city which is built on a promontory which juts out into the Atlantic. It has a long history as an important seaport. Cadiz was founded in about 1100 B.C. by the Phoenicians and many people think it is the oldest city in Europe. Christopher Columbus started two of his voyages from the city. Today Cadiz has a population of more than 150,000 and is famous for its February Carnival, which …

B **Examiner:** Was it a nice place to grow up?
Candidate: It was a great place to grow up. The climate is fantastic – really warm – so you can be out of doors most of the year round and it's a really safe environment too, so parents tend to be quite relaxed about letting the kids play unsupervised. And we had a lot of family and friends nearby – so it was a really happy time. There's also a great deal of natural beauty and a huge variety of plants and animals – and lots and lots of things for young people to do and be interested in.

C **Examiner:** Do you come from a town, village or city?
Candidate: I'm from Mussoorie originally. That's what we call a hill station. It's actually in the foothills of the Himalayas, in the north of India. It's not a big town, really. My parents still live there, although I've lived in Mumbai now for many years. So I suppose you could say I'm a small town boy who's also at home in the big city!

D **Examiner:** What do you do?
Candidate: I'm a doctor. That's why I am taking IELTS. I need to get Band 7 so I can continue my professional studies and qualify to practise medicine in this country. Actually, I am a well-respected, experienced professional in my own country, but I have to re-qualify in order to work here and unless I score 7 in all parts of IELTS I will eventually have to return home without working here at all. That would effectively end my hopes of developing my career further.

E **Examiner:** Was it a nice place to grow up?
Candidate: Yes.

F **Examiner:** What sports do you enjoy watching?
Candidate: Well, to tell you the truth, I'm not a very sporty person – somehow sports have never really caught my imagination. I watch the odd event with friends or family – the Olympics, maybe – but in fact the part I enjoy best is the opening and closing ceremonies, rather than the Games themselves! But if people I like being with are watching a football game, I'll sometimes watch with them.

2 Think about how you could improve the weaker answers. Make a few notes. Compare your notes with the comments on page 115.

3 Re-write the weaker answers. Try to produce a really good response to the question. Then look at the suggestions on page 115.

4 Give answers which are true for you to the following questions. Record your answers, or work with a partner.

1 Are you a student?
2 What do you like doing in your free time?
3 Are there any hobbies you enjoy?
4 Do you like travelling?
5 Are there any sports you don't enjoy?

Identifying strengths and weaknesses

1 21–26 Listen to six interviews from Part 1 of the Speaking test. Comment on the candidates' strengths and weaknesses and on how their performances could be improved. Use the checklist below and the Recording scripts on pages 123–124 to help you.

Checklist for good answers
- Do they answer the question directly?
- Do they just answer the question or do they say a bit more? Do they say enough in answer to each question?
- How fluent are they? How comfortable do they sound in English? Do they hesitate a lot?
- Do they organize what they say?
- How correct is their language?
- How much variety is there in the vocabulary and grammar structures they use? How natural does it sound?
- How easy is it to understand their pronunciation?

---

2 Record yourself answering the same questions. Listen to the recording and use the checklist above to help you evaluate your performance. If you have an English-speaking friend, ask them to listen and help with your evaluation.

Your turn

Use the prompts below to practise for Part 1 of the Speaking test. Imagine this is your IELTS Speaking test and follow all the prompts until you finish. Remember this part of the test is not more than five minutes including the introductions. If you are working with a friend, interview each other using one set of questions each. The interviewer should time the session. Record the interview and evaluate it using the checklist above. If you are working alone, use the second set of prompts for another practice session later.

Prompts 1

Do you come from a town, village or city?
Was it a nice place to grow up?
Do you think cities are improving, generally?

What subject are you studying?
Why did you choose that subject?
Is it hard?

Do you like doing any sports? Which?
What sports do you enjoy watching?
Are there any sports you don't like?

Prompts 2

What kind of food is popular where you come from?
Do you enjoy cooking?
Tell me about any food you don't like.

What kind of work do you do?
Why did you choose that?
Is it hard?

What sort of films do you like?
What do you most enjoy about that sort of film?
Tell me about a film you don't like.

True or False?

If the interviewer interrupts you often, it probably means you'll get a bad result.

Answer: This isn't necessarily true but it may mean you need to work on saying just a little less in answer to her questions. If you're still talking after 30 seconds, that's almost certainly too much.

Part 2

What happens

In Part 2 the examiner will give you a topic to talk about for 1–2 minutes. Before you speak you'll have one minute to think about what you want to say.

The examiner gives you a card with a topic on it. It will look like this:

Sample topic 1

Describe a letter you once received or wrote which was important to you.

Talk about:
- who it was to/from
- what it said
- what was special about it

and explain why it is still important to you today.

After one minute, the examiner will ask you to start speaking. You can start sooner than one minute if you like, but make sure you know what you're going to say first.

If you are still speaking after two minutes, the examiner will interrupt you. (This is not a problem.)

Planning your answer

You can make notes. The examiner will give you a pencil and paper.

1 Look at **Sample topic 1** again. Underline the key words and then check your answers on page 116.

2 Now do the same with **Sample topic 2** below. Again, see page 116 to check your answers.

Sample topic 2

Describe a machine you own which is important to you.

Talk about:
- what it is
- how you got it
- what you use it for

and explain why it is important to you.

---

3 🔘 27 Listen to the extract from Part 2 of the Speaking test. What do you think of the candidate's performance? In particular, does he answer all four questions relevantly?

Exam tip
Look at the sample topics again. There are four questions.
- The first two ask you to describe information.
- The second two ask you to explain something.

Notice that the second two are more interesting questions which will allow you to show off your English better than the first two. Make sure you leave enough time for them.

4 Choose one of the sample topics above. Use your key words and make one-word notes about each point.

5 Now use your notes to help you speak for 1–2 minutes. Time yourself. If you are working with a friend, time each other. The 'Candidate' should speak and the 'Examiner' should say nothing (just listen and time the candidate). After 60 seconds raise your hand silently to show the candidate that one minute has passed. If they are still speaking after two minutes, stop them.

Saying enough

Did you answer all the questions? Did you keep going for one minute? Two minutes? Remember, one minute is not a long time.

How to make sure you say enough
- Look at each of the key words. Think of three things to say about them.
- Write one word to remind you of each of those ideas.
- Make sure you describe everything you're asked about in the first two questions.
- Make sure you explain everything relevant in the second two questions.
- Remember to include your feelings and impressions as well as information.

Practise saying enough using sample topics 3 and 4 below.

Sample topic 3
Describe a place you have visited which impressed you.

Talk about:
- where this place is and how you travelled there
- what it is like
- why you went there
  and explain why it made an impression on you.

Sample topic 4
Describe a person you have met who made an impression on you.

Talk about:
- who they were
- how you met them
- what this person was like
  and explain why they impressed you.

Identifying strengths and weaknesses

🔘 28–30 Listen to three candidates answering Sample topic 3. Make notes on the candidates' strengths and weaknesses. Use the checklist below to help you. After listening, compare your notes with the comments on page 116.

> **Checklist for good answers**
> - Do they answer the four questions directly?
> - Do they just answer the question or do they say a bit more? Do they say enough in answer to each question? Do they speak for at least 60 seconds?
> - How fluent are they? How comfortable do they sound in English? Do they hesitate a lot?
> - Do they organize what they say?
> - How correct is their language?
> - How much variety is there in the vocabulary and grammar structures they use? How natural does it sound?
> - How easy is it to understand their pronunciation?

Your turn

Use Sample topics 5 and 6 to practise for Part 2 of the Speaking test. Follow steps 1–3 for one topic. Then repeat steps 1–3 with the second topic.

Look at the *Useful language* box on page 84 before you start.

> **Sample topic 5**
> Describe your first school.
>
> Talk about:
> - what kind of school it was
> - what it was like
> - whether you liked it and why (not)
>   and explain what importance it has had in your life.

> **Sample topic 6**
> Describe a celebration you have seen or taken part in which impressed you.
>
> Talk about:
> - what kind of celebration it was and why it took place
> - what it was like
> - how people felt during the celebration
>   and explain why it made an impression on you.

1 Preparing

Give yourself one minute to prepare. Decide early in the 60 seconds what you will talk about and spend most of the time making notes about the topic.

2 Speaking

Record yourself or ask a friend to listen to you, preferably someone who has a different first language or a native English speaker.

3 Evaluation

Use the checklist above. Ask a friend if they agree with your evaluation.

Remember
- Find the key words.
- Think of at least three things to say about each of the four questions. Make one-word notes.
- Leave enough time to talk about the more interesting third and fourth questions.
- Be careful that you don't develop a set of 'learned' answers. They will sound 'ready-made' and may not be relevant to the question you get in the exam.

Exam tip
When you listen to your recording, use a watch to check how long you spoke for. If you need to increase (or even reduce) how long you talk for, this will help you learn to do it.

I'd like to talk about a ...	(which) I	(once) ... used to ...

I first ...	when ... through ... by accident

What's more ...

The [funny/interesting/ridiculous] thing was ...

One of the [most interesting/frustrating/surprising] things about [him/her] was ...

I particularly remember ...

What I most remember about [him/her] is ...

It turned out that ...

Exam tip
This question is a way to finish Part 2 and lead into Part 3. You don't need to say much in response (unless you talked for a very short time in Part 2.).

Part 3

Follow-up questions

At the end of Part 2 the interviewer will ask you a follow-up question.

31–33 Listen to three follow-up questions and answers. Which answers are appropriate and why? Compare your ideas with the comments on page 116.

What happens

The examiner will ask you questions related to the topic in Part 2. However, the questions in Part 3 are of a more general nature (in Part 2 you discussed something concrete). There is more room to develop your answers than in Part 1, so don't feel you should stop speaking after a certain time. The examiner can interrupt with another question if they wish.

Possible topics

If the Part 2 topic is an important letter, then in Part 3 there could be questions about how people communicate with each other in general. Here are some possible questions:

- How do you generally communicate with friends and family?
- How do those methods compare with the ways in which your grandparents communicated?
- What are the advantages of the methods we use today?
- Do you think the methods your grandparents used to communicate have any advantages over the ways we use?
- If the 'speed of life' today is faster than ever before, is that a good thing?
- Do you think it's true that people today generally experience more stress than 50 or 100 years ago?
- How have communications changed in your lifetime?
- Technology gives us the chance to communicate more easily than people ever have before. What kinds of difficulties do we still have in communicating with each other?
- What causes those difficulties, do you think?

What makes a good answer

Part 3 gives you the chance to show how good your English is because you have more opportunity to talk about reasons, ideas, feelings and so on.

Identifying strengths and weaknesses

34–36 Listen to three candidates answering questions in Part 3. Make notes on the candidates' strengths and weaknesses. Use the checklist below to help you. After listening, compare your notes with the comments on page 117.

> **Checklist for good answers**
> - Do the candidates answer the question?
> - Do they talk about general issues?
> - Do they talk about their own attitudes?
> - Do they give reasons for their viewpoints?
> - Do they give specific examples and details to support their general ideas?
> - Do they say enough?

> **Saying enough – how do I know?**
> The key to this is:
> - Answer the question.
> - Explain why you think and feel as you do.
> - Give examples and details to support your general ideas.

> **Remember**
> - Describe your attitudes.
> - Explain why you think and feel as you do.
> - Give examples and details.
> - Be prepared to talk about things where you may not be sure of all the answers and to speculate a little.
> - Use this part of the Speaking test to show that you can discuss abstract issues.

Your turn

Use the questions below to practise for Part 3 of the Speaking test.

Record yourself and use the checklist above to evaluate your performance. If you are working with a friend, use the questions to interview each other.

Look at the *Useful language* box before you start.

Useful language

Explaining and justifying your point of view
On the whole …/In general …/I think in most cases …
I think there are [two/several] reasons for [that]. First … And second …
One example of that is …
That's why I feel that …

Suggesting and speculating
I think one reason for [that] may be …
It may be a good idea to …
It may be worth … [+ *ing* or noun phrase]

Adding things and moving on
As well as that …
Not only that but …
As far as … is concerned …

Comparing and contrasting
It's quite similar to …
It's almost as … as …
They're not as … as …
It's far more … than …
Having said that … (= On the other hand …)
Although, that said, …

Questions on people

1 Who have been some of the most important people in your life?
2 Do you think that public people – leaders, sports people and other role models – are as important in our lives as the people we know?
3 Do you think it's true that we choose friends who agree with us?
4 Are there any fictional characters who have been important influences in your life?
5 What are your own strongest and weakest characteristics, do you think?
6 Do you think it's possible for people to change?

Questions on schools and education

1 Would you be happy for your children to receive the same education that you did?
2 In what ways could it be improved?
3 Should schools focus on academic skills and knowledge, or are there other areas they should work on?
4 Was it your school which taught you the most important lessons of your life?
5 Is education something that stops when you leave school or university?

Practice test

Section 1   Questions 1–10

 37

Questions 1–6

Complete the notes below. Write **NO MORE THAN THREE WORDS AND/OR A NUMBER** for each answer.

Library – New member's details

First name: Mahmoud

Surname: **1** ALNIZRI

Address: **2** 195 Hills Road

Postcode: unknown

Telephone: **3** 07942 116470

Membership type: Individual Student Membership

Fees: Free membership

Students must pay for:
- ordering books from storage;
- borrowing   **4** CDs AND DVD-

Book request

You have ordered this book: Listening Skills for Students

Fee: **5** $ 50

Reference number: **6** ABC 096109

Questions 7–10

Label the rooms on the plan of the library. Choose your labels from the box on the left.

Plan of Library

A Toilets
B Main reading room
C Stairs
D Main computer suite
E Canteen
F Smokers' room

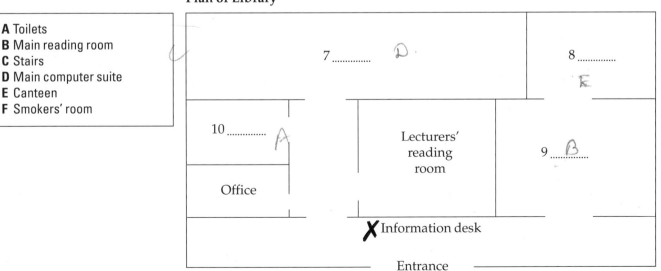

Section 2   Questions 11–20

 38

Questions 11–15

Circle the appropriate letter.

11 The most frequent cause of anxiety for international students is usually
    A English language.
    B money problems.
    C getting to know people.

12 Often the biggest problem in the first week is
    A making friends.
    B feeling bewildered.
    C getting lost.

13 In the past the most worrying issue at the end of the year has been
    A socializing.
    B academic performance.
    C finding a job.

14 The speaker thinks that during the first week the students should concentrate on
    A mixing with people.
    B going to lectures.
    C English lessons.

15 The most convenient form of transport is
    A a bicycle.
    B the bus.
    C on foot.

Questions 16–20

Complete the table. Use **NO MORE THAN THREE WORDS** for each answer.

	Week 1 events for international students		
	English language support	Managing your money	Clubs and societies
Type of event	(16)	lecture	(19) Interesting
Advice	Use language centre (17) computer in spare time. laboratory	(18) open bank o/c.	(20) Enthos native newsletter

Section 3   Questions 21–30

 39

Questions 21–26

What suggestions does Dr Poole have for Richard about learning Chinese? Choose your answers from the box and write the letters **A–C** next to questions **21–26**.

A Do immediately
B Do in the future
C No need to do at all

21 Get new books,
22 Improve pronunciation.
23 Go abroad.
24 Work on grammar.
25 Practise writing.
26 Expand vocabulary.

Questions 27–30

Complete the sentences. Write **NO MORE THAN THREE WORDS** for each answer.

27 Dr Poole thinks Richard's biggest need is to improve his ....

28 She thinks Richard could develop his written Chinese by attending
    .... with Chinese students.

29 Richard can improve his understanding of Chinese structures by reading
    ....

30 If he goes to the China Society meetings and watches television he can practise his
    ....

Section 4   Questions 31–40

🔊 40

Questions 31–32

Circle the appropriate letter.

31 The earliest known use of hot springs for bathing was in
    A Finland.
    B Japan.
    C Greece.

32 Leisure centres are a
    A Roman invention.
    B Japanese invention.
    C modern invention.

Questions 33–37

Complete the sentences. Write **NO MORE THAN TWO WORDS AND/OR A NUMBER** for each answer.

33 The Romans developed a British spa at ....

34 The water temperature there is about .... Celsius.

35 Spas again became popular in Europe in the ....

36 There were spas in Germany, France, ... and Britain.

37 More than two centuries ago doctors recommended drinking spa water for
    ....

Questions 38–40

Circle the appropriate letter.

38 Some people believe that skin conditions are improved by spa waters
    A high in carbonated salts.
    B high in sulphur.
    C from the mains water supply.

39 The speaker says bottled water is
    A reasonably priced.
    B healthier than tap water.
    C big business.

40 The speaker says water will become a major geopolitical issue
    A in the next ten years.
    B during the 21st century.
    C in the next few years.

You should spend about 20 minutes on **Questions 1–13**, which are based on Reading Passage 1.

Why computer games are good for your child

A The idea of bringing computer games in the classroom seems likely to provoke more detentions than learning. But that's slowly changing. To some, children may be playing *SimCity*; to others, they are learning geography. To some, they are playing fantasy football; to others, they are learning maths and strategy skills. Gaming, whether online, on a console or on a computer, is thought by many teachers and parents to be the classic signs of a modern wasted youth. Where once it was snooker halls, now it's Lara Croft and her legions of imitators as the classic signs of a life frittered away.

B But some educationalists beg to differ, saying that gaming extends and improves a whole range of skills and aptitudes and can benefit learning. Indeed, in a survey for the technology and investment company Nesta Futurelab earlier this year, a third of teachers are already using computer games and believe they improve skills. Out of the survey of 1000 teachers, 91% thought they developed motor and cognitive skills, and 60% believed they would develop thinking skills and acquire specific knowledge. We are faced with a gaming generation of children who spend their time and money on online and computer games. At the very least, this makes them technically literate – often more so than their teachers, who can feel embarrassed on occasion by a perceived lack of skills compared to the kids in front of them. A report by the University of Bristol found that teachers were happy using computers at home, but would not take the risk of getting it wrong in front of a class of pupils and, partly as a result, some 30% of teachers surveyed failed to make good use of computers in the classroom. But there is a growing feeling that games can be useful learning tools and do, in fact, help children develop their mental agility and even build social skills (children prefer gaming in small groups). For one thing, as any adult who has tried them will tell you, the games themselves are actually hard, requiring a significant number of skills – hand-eye coordination, multi-tasking, strategy and the management of complex variables, communication, literacy and problem-solving, on top of the computer skills necessary.

C Specific games can be used for specific subjects – schools do use *SimCity* (the simulation planning and strategy game), either as special education versions or as the commercial product, to help teach geography. Others prefer to use games developed specifically for learning purposes. Researchers at the technology developers Nesta Futurelab have, for example, developed *Astroversity*, a space rescue mission that gets children to collaborate in order to rescue victims after a

disaster in a space station. Even a football management game requires the ability to interrogate huge databases of information and make complex decisions. And usually without the child noticing.

D And that can be the beauty of games in the classroom – the problem of motivating students can disappear when they are confronted with familiar and enjoyable tasks. It becomes far less difficult to persuade them to work on their own and even in their own time. Pride and satisfaction become drivers in motivating children to perform well against each other and provide a way for children to interact with each other (off-screen) with gaming leagues and the like. Of course, assessment of games-based coursework can be difficult (not least if you insist that it isn't the winning that matters) and the application of games to the national curriculum can be tenuous.

E But they can also be used as a springboard for class discussion on issues which are on the list of learning objectives. Games such as *The Sims* can prompt discussions on areas of citizenship and government and on areas of science such as pollution, energy and global warming. Complex strategic decisions in planning games are best discussed as a class and the creation of a *SimCity*, for example, involves building a well-thought out infrastructure. Should it fail, the software gives instant feedback (in the form of a newspaper) and pupils learn instantly how their thoughts have succeeded or not, and can therefore discuss it and rethink for next time. The trick is to stop the thought processes that see the games as an end in themselves and keep plugging the games back into the real world and the curriculum.

F Of course, trying to co-opt games into the classroom is not without problems. For one, the games are built to obsess users – getting them so absorbed that turning away is a real problem. Engagement can be great – up to a point. Getting children to turn back to mainstream educational methods can be difficult and introducing such a youth culture into the classroom can be an issue – pupils may take it less seriously and parents could be horrified. The selection of games too can be an issue. But gaming companies and schools are already working together on a project called *Teaching with Games* which will test the use of commercial computer games *The Sims* and its follow-ups, *RollerCoaster* and *Knights of Honour*, and help develop lesson plans to support the use of these and other games. It is due to conclude at the end of this year. By then, we may already be further on the road to blurring the edges between gaming and learning just a little more.

Questions 1–5

Reading Passage 1 has six paragraphs **A–F**. Which paragraph contains the following information?
NB You may use any letter more than once.

> 1 How playing computer games can make students work more willingly
> 2 An example of cooperation between computer game businesses and education authorities
> 3 Some difficulties in using computer games in schools
> 4 A description of traditional attitudes towards computer games
> 5 The uses of some games specially designed for education purposes

Questions 6–9

Complete the summary of Paragraph B. Choose **NO MORE THAN THREE WORDS** from Paragraph B for each answer.

Computer games are thought to contribute positively to learning by developing children's (6) .... More than nine out of ten teachers questioned believed that children can increase their (7) ....
skills through gaming. A fear of appearing less (8) .... than the children they teach prevents many teachers from using computers in the classroom. Because children like to interact with each other with computer games they can also increase their (9) .... skills while they approach intricate problems with sophisticated tactics.

Questions 10–13

Do the following statements agree with the information given in Paragraphs A and B of the text? Write:

TRUE   if the statement agrees with the information in the text
FALSE   if the statement contradicts the information in the text
NOT GIVEN   if the text contains no information about the statement

10 The image of computer games in children's learning is improving.
11 Parents are now ready to welcome computer games into the classroom.
12 Few teachers think computer games will teach children any particular information.
13 Games provide an encouraging new way to test what children have learned.

Reading Passage 2

You should spend about 20 minutes on **Questions 14–26**, which are based on Reading Passage 2.

Cruel to be kind

1 Would you let another driver into your lane in heavy traffic? Or are you the sort of driver who slows to a crawl when someone is tailgating or driving much too close behind you? If you do either, it's OK: you're only being human.

2 To date, no evidence either of altruism or spite has been found in any other animal except *Homo sapiens*. Being nice or nasty at a cost to yourself could be part of what makes you human. But now scientists are investigating our closest genetic relative, the chimpanzee. Somewhere in the 99.7 per cent of DNA that the two species share, perhaps there are genes for charity and malice.

3 In a study carried out at Germany's Max Planck Institute for Evolutionary Anthropology, which was published in the British journal *Proceedings of the Royal Society* in 2006, researchers tested whether chimpanzees would help or hinder a hungry neighbour. A chimpanzee in a testing room had two choices: it could either deliver food to a chimpanzee in a room next door, or to an empty room. In both cases, the chimpanzee controlling the food could not get any itself.

The study found the chimpanzee controlling the food would do nothing for half the time, then give food to the other chimpanzee only a quarter of the time – which demonstrates neither altruism nor spite. 'I was predicting chimps would be spiteful,' says Keith Jensen, a doctoral student who led the study. 'I mean, they're chimpanzees. I get spat on all the time. But though they knew they couldn't get the food, sometimes they gave it to the other guy anyway.'

4 In contrast, humans frequently perform selfless acts. We donate blood, give money to charities and help old ladies cross the street. Altruism is among the very foundations of our society. Banking, government, and health services all depend on people working for the benefit of complete strangers.

5 And we can be spiteful too. In the famous *Ultimatum Game*, $10 is to be shared by two people. Person 1 decides how the $10 is to be split between them, and Person 2 chooses to accept or reject the offer. If the offer is rejected, neither gets anything. Economists predicted Person 1 would offer a $9/$1 split and that Person 2 would accept it because $1 is better than nothing. Surprisingly, Person 1 generally offers a kind and fair $5/$5 split, which is accepted. If anything less even is offered, Person 2 generally rejects the offer, docking their own pay as punishment for the other person's selfishness.

6 What happens if chimpanzees are rewarded? In a similar study published in *Nature* in October 2005, the chimpanzee controlling the food received food regardless of whether or not it chose to deliver food to a neighbour or an empty room. Again, the chimpanzee in control gave food to the neighbour only about a quarter of the time – even when the other chimpanzee was begging frantically.

7 If able to help others at no cost to themselves, most humans will do so. This is called 'other-regarding', which means humans are considerate to each other. Chimps, it seems, are not. 'I don't know why chimps are not other-regarding,' says Joan Silk from the University of California at Los Angeles, who led the study. 'It might be they are unaware of others' needs. It might be they are aware, but unconcerned.' The findings may come as a surprise to field primatologists who often observe chimpanzees sharing food in the wild, even precious sources of protein like meat. 'Food sharing among adults in the wild might be based on self-interest,' says Silk. 'Males might share meat with other males because they anticipate receiving meat in return in the future. Alternatively, males might share meat because it is more costly to monopolise it than to allow others to share it.'

8 But for now it appears humans are the only animals known to think considerately and inconsiderately about others even when they are strangers. Chimpanzees do not appear to have either the ability or the inclination. Perhaps somewhere along the split with our common ancestor, the selfless gene and the mean gene evolved.

9 So next time someone cuts into your lane, relax – it's higher evolution at work.

Questions 14–17

Match each researcher or piece of research (Questions **14–17**) with the correct finding (**A–H**) from the box below.
NB There are more findings than research/researchers so you will not use them all.

14 German researchers
15 Research based on an economics game
16 Research published in *Nature*
17 Joan Silk

List of findings
A A chimpanzee's behaviour is not affected by whether the chimp itself has food.
B People often do generous things.
C Studying chimpanzees has revealed much about how humans drive.
D People normally put their own interests first.
E Chimpanzee behaviour demonstrates neither generosity nor meanness.
F Generosity and meanness may be determined by our genes.
G Chimpanzees will steal food when they can.
H We simply do not understand why chimps behave differently from people.

Questions 18–22

Circle the appropriate letter.

18 The genetic differences between humans and chimpanzees are
    A well-understood.
    B being studied.
    C 99.7% understood.
    D not measurable.

19 Keith Jensen was surprised by the result of his research because
    A chimpanzees are known to be kindly creatures.
    B he has experienced chimpanzees being unfriendly to him.
    C chimpanzees usually share food with each other.
    D he predicted that the hungry chimpanzee would get the food.

20 According to the writer, some social institutions are examples of human
    A foolishness.
    B generosity.
    C welfare.
    D selfishness.

21 According to the writer, the results of the *Ultimatum Game* showed that people generally
    A penalize unjust treatment.
    B accept unjust treatment.
    C expect unjust treatment.
    D enjoy unjust treatment.

22 According to Joan Silk, in normal circumstances, chimpanzees frequently
    A understand each other's needs.
    B feel concern about each other's needs.
    C meet each other's needs.
    D ignore each other's needs.

Questions 23–26

Complete the sentences with words from Reading Passage 2. Write **NO MORE THAN THREE WORDS** for each answer.

23 The chimpanzee is humankind's ....

24 Many human social institutions rely on people helping ....

25 Anthropologists call creatures which consider others' needs ....

26 A .... gene may be responsible for our unkind behaviour.

You should spend about 20 minutes on **Questions 27–40**, which are based on Reading Passage 3.

All about hypnosis

A The popular representation of hypnosis – the mysterious hypnotist figure popularized in movies, comic books and television – bears little resemblance to actual hypnotism. In fact, modern understanding of hypnosis contradicts this conception on several key points. Subjects in a hypnotic trance are not slaves to their 'masters' – they have absolute free will. And they're not really in a semi-sleep state – they're actually hyperattentive.

B The phenomenon of hypnosis is still a mystery of sorts, but psychiatrists do have some model of how it works. It is a trance state characterized by extreme suggestibility, relaxation and heightened imagination. It's not really like sleep, because the subject is alert the whole time. It is most often compared to daydreaming, or the feeling of 'losing yourself' in a book or movie. You are fully conscious, but you tune out most of the stimuli around you. You focus intently on the subject at hand, to the near exclusion of any other thought. This deep hypnosis is often compared to the relaxed mental state between wakefulness and sleep.

In conventional hypnosis, you approach the suggestions of the hypnotist, or your own ideas, as if they were reality. If the hypnotist suggests that you are drinking a chocolate milkshake, you'll taste the milkshake and feel it cooling your mouth and throat. If the hypnotist suggests that you are afraid, you may feel panicky or start to sweat. But the entire time, you are aware that it's all imaginary. Essentially, you're 'playing pretend' on an intense level, as kids do.

In this special mental state, people are highly suggestible. That is, when the hypnotist tells you to do something, you'll probably embrace the idea completely. This is what makes stage hypnotist shows so entertaining. Normally reserved, sensible adults are suddenly walking around the stage clucking like chickens or singing at the top of their lungs. Fear of embarrassment seems to fly out the window. The subject's sense of safety and morality remain entrenched throughout the experience, however. A hypnotist can't get you to do anything you don't want to do.

C The predominant school of thought on hypnosis is that it is a way to access a person's subconscious mind directly. Normally, you are only aware of the thought processes in your conscious mind. You consciously think over the problems that are right in front of you, consciously choose words as you speak, consciously try to remember where you left your keys.

But in doing all these things, your conscious mind is working hand-in-hand with your subconscious mind, the unconscious part of your mind that does your 'behind the scenes' thinking. Your subconscious mind accesses the vast reservoir of information that lets you solve problems, construct sentences or locate your keys. It puts together plans and ideas and runs them by your conscious mind. When a new idea comes to you out of the blue, it's because you already thought through the process unconsciously. In short, your subconscious mind does most of your thinking, and it decides a lot of what you do. When you're awake, your conscious mind works to evaluate a lot of these thoughts, make decisions and put certain ideas into action. It also processes new information and relays it to the subconscious mind. But when you're asleep, the conscious mind gets out of the way, and your subconscious has free reign.

Psychiatrists theorize that the deep relaxation and focusing exercises of hypnotism work to calm and subdue the conscious mind so that it takes a less active role in your thinking process. In this state, you're still aware of what's going on, but your conscious mind takes a back seat to your subconscious mind. Effectively, this allows you and the hypnotist to work directly with the subconscious. It's as if the hypnotism process pops open a control panel inside your brain.

D The most widespread example of hypnotic behavioural modification is habit-control hypnotic treatment. In this application, a hypnotist focuses on one particular habit that is embedded in your unconscious (smoking or overeating, for example). With the 'control panel' to your mind open, the hypnotist may be able to reprogram your subconscious to reverse the behaviour. Some hypnotists do this by connecting a negative response with the bad habit. For example, the hypnotist might suggest to your subconscious that smoking will cause nausea. If this association is programmed effectively, you will feel sick every time you think about smoking a cigarette. Alternatively, the hypnotist may build up your will power, suggesting to your subconscious that you don't need cigarettes, and you don't want them.

E One form of psychiatric hypnotherapy involves bringing underlying psychiatric problems up to the conscious level. Accessing fears, memories and repressed emotions can help to clarify difficult issues and bring resolution to persistent problems.

A controversial form of hypnotism is medical hypnotherapy. Doctors and spiritual leaders all over the world claim that hypnotic suggestion can ease pain and even cure illness in some patients. The underlying idea behind this is that the mind and body are inextricably intertwined. When you suggest to the subconscious that the body does not feel pain, or that the body is free of disease, the subconscious may actually bring about the change.

The success of hypnotherapy is undeniable, but many doctors argue it's clear that the mind can influence all aspects of the physical body, so it makes sense that a firmly held belief can reduce pain or even help treat a disease. In the end, this explanation of hypnosis amounts to pretty much the same thing as the trance theory. When you absolutely convince somebody that you've brought about a change in their subconscious, they register this information as a fact. So, even if the hypnotic state is nothing more than a figment of the subject's imagination, hypnotic suggestions can still reform their deeply held beliefs.

Questions 27–31

Reading Passage 3 has five sections **A–E**. Choose the correct heading for each section from the list of headings in the box.

> **List of headings**
> 1 The healing power of the subconscious mind
> 2 Two levels of mental activity
> 3 The power of addictions
> 4 Behaviour modification
> 5 What happens under hypnosis
> 6 Hypnosis in history
> 7 An inaccurate understanding
> 8 Hypnosis and emotions

27 Section A ....
28 Section B ....
29 Section C ....
30 Section D ....
31 Section E ....

Questions 32–36

Do the following statements agree with the information given in Paragraphs 1 and 2 of Reading Passage 3? Write:

YES   if the statement agrees with the claims of the writer
NO   if the statement contradicts the claims of the writer
NOT GIVEN   if it is impossible to say what the writer thinks about this

32 The distinction between reality and imagination becomes unclear during hypnosis.
33 Hypnotic subjects can be persuaded to do things they would normally disapprove of.
34 It is thought that hypnotism reduces the activity of the conscious mind.
35 Hypnosis is among the most successful ways of giving up smoking.
36 There is no doubt that hypnotherapy is effective.

Questions 37–40

Complete the sentences. Choose **NO MORE THAN TWO WORDS** from Reading Passage 3 for each answer.

37 The main difference between being asleep and been hypnotized is that during hypnosis you are always ....
38 Stage hypnotist shows demonstrate that people are extremely .... under hypnosis.
39 One way to modify an undesirable habit is to link it subconsciously to a
   ....
40 Hypnosis is thought to reduce pain because our mental and physical beings are
   ....

Writing Task 1

You should spend about 20 minutes on this task.

The chart below shows the proportions of one country's main energy supplies derived from different sources in 2006.

Summarize the information by selecting and reporting the main features and make comparisons where relevant.

Write at least 150 words.

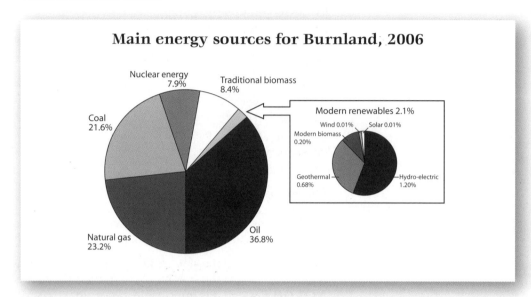

Writing Task 2

You should spend about 40 minutes on this task.

Write about the following topic.

Rapid advances are being made in medical treatments of different kinds. Many people think governments should provide these treatments free to their citizens.

To what extent do you agree or disagree with this point of view?

Give reasons for your answer and include any relevant examples from your own knowledge or experience.

Write at least 250 words.

Part 1

The examiner asks you some general questions about yourself, your home, your job or your studies. For example:

- What do you like doing in your free time?
- What sports do you enjoy watching?
- Do you enjoy exercise? What sort?
- Tell me about the place where you live.
- Talk about a film you have enjoyed. Why did you like it?
- What sort of food do you like?
- Do you like travelling?

Part 2

The examiner gives you a card with questions similar to those below. You have one minute to think about the topic and make notes if you wish. You should then talk about the topic for 1–2 minutes.

Talk about a town or city you like. You should say:
- what kind of town or city it is
- how you know this place
- the things you enjoy doing there
and explain what it is about the place that you like so much.

When you have finished, the examiner may ask you one or two questions about what you have said. For example:

- When did you last go there?
- Do you know anyone who is there now?

Part 3

The examiner will ask you some discussion questions related to the topic in Part 2. For example:

- Do you think cities are changing for the better, generally?
- Why do you think more and more people are living in cities?
- What are some of the benefits and disadvantages of living in the countryside?
- Do you think it is important to know and visit the places where your parents, grandparents and other ancestors lived?

Answer key

Quiz p. 7

1 A 4
   B 1
   C 3
   D 2
2 A, B, D, E, F, G, I, J
3 British, American, Australian, New Zealand
4 ONCE

Section 1 p. 7

Skills development p. 7

Prediction p. 8

1 1 two speakers
   2 travel/transport

2 1 the name of a town
   2 a number, day, week or month
   3 the name of a town
   4 a number
   5 a means of transport

Completing notes p. 8

1 Harrogate
2 next week/next week sometime/sometime next week
3 Leeds
4 three
5 by coach/by bus

Skills development p. 8

1 6 a day (*on* + a day)
   7 a time (*at* + a time)
   8 a type of ticket
   9 and 12   a length of time
   10 and 11   a time (*at* + a time)

2 6 C
   7 A, C
   8 A, B, C
   9 and 12   C, D
   10 and 11   A, B, E

Completing a sentence p. 9

6 Thursday
7 2.00 pm/14.00/two o'clock
8 one way
9 2 hours 45 minutes
10 two thirty/2.30
11 2.00 pm/14.00/two o'clock
12 6 hours 35 minutes

Skills development p. 9

Completing a table p. 9

1 **Table 1**: booking a flight, travelling by air, going on holiday
   Table 2: subscribing to digital TV

2 **Table 1:**
   1 and 2 numbers
   3 days of the week, months, times of day
   4 letters, numbers
   Table 2:
   1 length of time, months, years
   2 numbers
   3 numbers, names
   4 numbers

3 13 **Young Traveller's Railcard**
   14 25%
   15 £18.75
   16 £10

Skills development p. 10

Listening for letters and numbers

1 B C D E G P T V   /iː/
   A H J K   /eɪ/
   F L M N S X Z   /e/
   I Y   /aɪ/
   O   /əʊ/
   R   /ɑː/
   Q U W   /juː/

2 1 0870 225225
   2 6.5
   3 6.75
   4 6½
   5 9.20 pm
   6 9.45 am
   7 slash
   8 at
   9 dot

3 1 1998
   2 August 13th
   3 £40.14
   4 2½ hours
   5 97 miles
   6 1770
   7 7 hours
   8 2004

4 1 Euston
   2 Victoria
   3 HG2 1JL
   4 Fauvell
   5 Birmingham
   6 Warwick
   7 PB7 9RL
   8 Manchester

Completing notes and tables p.11

1 (the) High Street
2 Daunt
3 429 6241
4 Raddlebarn
5 £60
6 20%
7 £48
8 £20
9 £15
10 15%

Section 2 p.12

Skills development p. 12

Prediction p.12

1 at a university
2 a member of staff/a person in authority/an ex-student
   We can predict that it will be someone who is in a position
   to give information about the university.
3 new students
   Looking at the question *stems* (the information you are
   given in the question) – *The university is situated ... The
   individual colleges ...* – we can see that the information is
   descriptive, and probably useful in an induction talk.
4 Key words:
   1 university/situated
   2 colleges
   3 examinations/managed
   4 library/widest/collection
   These topics are in the question stems and we can be sure
   the talk will cover them.
5 1 situated/campus/town = location of the university
   2 colleges/university/separate/together/independent =
      relationship of the colleges to the university/each other
   3 examinations/managed/colleges/faculties/director
      of studies = university authorities responsible for
      examinations
   4 library/collection = library facilities across university
      institutions

Key words and synonyms p.12

1 located/to be found/sited
2 throughout/all around/in many parts/everywhere
3 separate/distinct/different/single
4 supervised/administered/controlled/organized
5 most comprehensive/most extensive/fullest
6 choice/range/quantity

Questions 1–4
1 B
2 B
3 C
4 C

Skills development p. 13

Steps i and ii
5 Which TWO of the following <u>services</u> are <u>provided</u> by the
   <u>Colleges</u>?

Step iii
Sports facilities
Academic direction   ✓
Counselling services
Accommodation   ✓
Health advice

Note: *sports facilities,
academic direction* and
accommodation are all
MENTIONED in the
talk. **But** ...

Step iv
The speaker uses a negative to make it clear that sports
facilities are not provided by the colleges: *There <u>aren't</u> any sports
facilities in the Colleges.*

Types of map questions: Revising locations and labelling a map p. 14

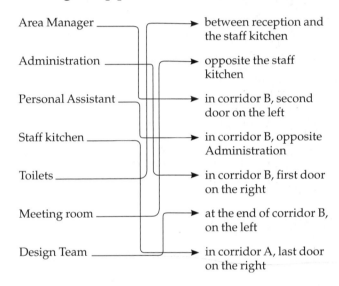

Area Manager ————————→ between reception and
                         the staff kitchen

Administration ————————→ opposite the staff
                         kitchen

Personal Assistant ——————→ in corridor B, second
                         door on the left

Staff kitchen ————————→ in corridor B, opposite
                         Administration

Toilets ——————————→ in corridor B, first door
                         on the right

Meeting room ————————→ at the end of corridor B,
                         on the left

Design Team ————————→ in corridor A, last door
                         on the right

Questions 6–10
6 Students' Union
7 Science Faculty
8 supermarket/university supermarket
9 sports centre
10 swimming pool

Skills development p. 15

Completing summaries p. 15

i   Key words: union/student/interests
ii Topic: university student unions/functions
iii Context: union/university
iv Grammatical possibilities: see text below. The words
    underlined are the <u>clues</u> to the grammatical possibilities.

The union is the centre of student (*noun*). It has <u>two</u> (*plural
noun*) and <u>a</u> (*singular noun*) at weekends. There <u>are</u> also
(*number/adjective*) clubs and (*plural noun*) that <u>encourage</u>
leisure activities.

The union's formal functions are <u>to</u> (*verb*) student interests. The executive is <u>responsible for</u> (*gerund/noun*) that affect students. In addition, they advance student (<u>0 article</u>) (*plural noun/adverb*) at university board meetings. The union executive works with (<u>0 article</u>) (*plural noun*) to foster positive relations between the university and the town. The local union collaborates with other (*plural noun*).

1 social life
2 bars
3 night club
4 sports
5 associations
6 represent
7 negotiating issues
8 concerns
9 local organizations
10 student unions

Section 3 p. 16

Skills development p. 16

Synonyms and paraphrasing p. 17

1 She gives interesting lectures/expresses herself clearly/has stimulating ideas.
2 His talks are rather boring, but he knows his subject well./His lectures are dull, but he's a famous specialist in his field.
3 Lively speaker, relevant content./Gives entertaining lectures, includes essential information.
4 He's sometimes brilliant/inspiring, but sometimes terrible/awful/dreadful.

Classifying questions p. 17

1 A
2 C
3 A
4 B

Skills practice

Dialogue 1

Questions 1–5
1 planned
2 made a list
3 a timetable
4 realistic
5 subjects

Questions 6–10
6 C
7 C
8 C
9 A
10 B

Dialogue 2

Questions 1–6
1 A
2 A
3 C
4 A
5 B
6 B

Short answer questions p. 18
7 the excitement
8 making a profit
9 (the) hard work
10 time-consuming
11 control the accounts
12 detailed business plan

Section 4 p. 18

Skills development p. 18

Understanding the question: Skimming p. 18

1 development/construction site logistics management
2 supplied/logistics management
3 big projects/controlled/site logistics management
4 benefits/logistics management/construction industry
5 career advantages/logistic management/individuals

Note: By skimming questions 1–5 you can see that 'logistics management' appears in every one and is therefore a central topic. This is a fairly technical term and, as you are not expected to have specialist knowledge in the IELTS listening test, it will be explained in the listening text. If an expression is unfamiliar to you, it is important to listen carefully at the beginning of the lecture to discover what it means.

Understanding the question: Scanning p. 19

Listen for:
1 THREE reasons
2 TWO services NOT supplied
3 THREE projects
4 TWO benefits for industry
5 TWO advantages NOT for individuals

Skills practice

Questions 1–5
1 A, B, E
2 B, E
3 B, D, E
4 B, D
5 A, C

Skills development p. 20

Signpost language p. 20

1 introducing/focusing on a new topic: C, E, K
2 tracing a chronological process: F, M
3 contrasting ideas: B, L, H
4 giving an example: G
5 indicating steps in a logical argument: D, I, N, O
6 indicating the structure of a lecture: A
7 referring to a previous comment: J

Questions 1–6
1 business sector
2 customer
3 Graduates
4 non-specialists
5 verticals
6 designer outlets

7   I
8   D
9   C
10 F

Key for Reading module

Quiz p. 22

1 True.
2 False. Write your answers directly onto the answer sheet.
3 False. There are three. Allow 20 minutes per text, minus a minute to skim the whole paper before you begin.
4 True. It's usually the third text.
5 True.
6 This is generally true.
7 False. Wrong spellings will cost you marks. Make sure you copy spellings correctly from the text. Not all questions are multiple choice.
8 False. You can choose. But make sure you write your answers in the correct boxes on the answer sheet.
9 False. Pencil only.
10 False.
11 False. You need to read more serious magazines and academic books.
12 False. This book will teach you the exam skills you need. You need to practise those skills until you can use them fast and easily. You also need to develop confidence in reading academic texts and a wide vocabulary. Regular reading of more serious magazines and academic books will give you an advantage. Using an exam preparation book is not enough on its own.

Reading Passage 1 p. 22

Skills development p. 22

Skimming p. 22

1

A World Bank, nutrition, economic growth

B internationally, malnutrition, nutrition, growth rates, poor countries

C malnutrition, poor countries

D nutrition, development, malnutrition

E international community, nutrition

F donor community, resources, technical and financial

Note: Some key words may be modified by prefixes, eg nutrition/malnutrition. Identifying these will give you a clearer focus on the aspect of the topic being discussed.

2
A

Matching headings to paragraphs p. 24

B 4
C 5
D 6
E 2

Skills development p. 24

Scanning for facts p. 24

Area/country/continent		% of child population affected	
		anaemic	malnourished
1	world	NG	30%
2	South Asia	NG	50%
3	Sub-Saharan Africa	NG	25%
4	India/high income	65%	NG
5	India/low income	88%	NG

Multiple-choice questions p. 24

1 D
2 D
3 A

Skills development p. 25

Guessing meaning from context p. 25

Proportion
Clues from the text: *more than half of all child deaths worldwide … 30% … 60%*
From these clues you could reasonably guess that proportion is connected with percentages and ratios.

Anaemic
Clues from the text: *26 per cent of children in the highest income bracket in India are underweight and 65 per cent are anaemic. Anaemic children perform less well in school, are more likely to drop out and have lower intellectual and physical productivity as adults.*
From these clues a reasonable guess is that anaemic relates to a damaging condition resulting from malnourishment.

Obesity
Clues from the text: Obesity is *the other side of malnutrition, which the developed world … faces*. It is *the overweight agenda*. It *links very closely to non-communicable disease like cardio-vascular heart disease, diabetes and cancers.*
From these clues you could reasonably guess that obesity is a result of overeating.

Funding
Clues from the text: *(financial) resources – invest – invest – co-finance* – and the fact that the reason given for funding is *to scale-up actions to prevent malnutrition.*
From these clues you could reasonably guess that funding is associated with financial matters.

Reading Passage 2 p. 26

1 D
2 B iii
3 C viii
4 D ix
5 E vii
6 F ii
7 G iv
8 D
9 C
10 A

Questions 11–13 – in any order:

11 A
12 E
13 F

14 position
15 interest
16 silence

Reading Passage 3 p. 28

Skills development p. 28

Summarizing and paraphrasing p.28

1 ice cap/ice sheet/glaciers
2 disintegrate/breakup/flooding/melting
3 faster/accelerating rate/speed/three times faster
4 dramatically/catastrophic/dramatic/disaster/

Matching statements to paragraphs p.28

1 A iii
2 B iv
3 C vii
4 D vi
5 E ii
6 B

Skills development p. 30

Scanning for opinions p. 30

1

1 scientists
2 scientists
3 Eric Rignot
4 we (scientists/the general public)
5 the latest study
6 scientists
7 researchers

Questions 7–12

7 C
8 B
9 A
10 A
11 B
12 C

2

A southern hemisphere
B the past ten years
C all/sea ports/world/disappear
D habitat/bacteria/animals
E more than half/sea-level/breaking up/not melting

Questions 13–14 – in either order:

13 B
14 E

A *southern hemisphere –* is not *mentioned in the text. The southern half of Greenland is mentioned.*
B *the past ten years/the last ten years*
C *(sea) ports – world –* not *mentioned in the text*
D *bacteria – animals – habitat –* not *mentioned in the text*
E *more than half/sealevel/breaking up/not melting*

15 lubricant
16 behaviour
17 disintegration
18 FALSE. Twice as much.
19 FALSE. Scientists believe that computer models of how the Greenland ice sheet will react to global warming have seriously underestimated the threat posed by sea levels.
20 TRUE. It formed over thousands of years by the gradual accumulation of ice and snow but now its disintegration could occur in decades or centuries.
21 NOT GIVEN.
22 NOT GIVEN. Scientists estimate that, in 1996, glaciers deposited about 50 cubic km of ice into the sea. In 2005 it had risen to 150 cubic km of ice.

Reading Passage 4 p. 32

Questions 1–20

1 D
2 J
3 F
4 E
5 I
6 B
7 thinkers
8 health
9 blood pressure
10 ethical
11 B
12 D
13 vegetarian diet
14 less fat
15 fibre
16 diet
17 coronary/heart disease
18 366
19 charities and education
20 early last century/1930

Reading Passage 5 p. 35

Identifying and comparing data on a chart p.35

1

i Living arrangements
ii Living in a couple/Not living in a couple
iii Percentage

Summary

2

1 partnership
2 10
3 31
4 29
5 1974

Skills development p. 36

1

C (Although D mentions the relative position of wives to single women, the first three paragraphs, and the majority of the article, focus on unmarried women and the fact that their numbers are increasing.)

2

Married women	Cohabitation
synonyms wives	synonyms living together
antonyms single women singletons unmarried women	antonyms living alone
associated expressions marry married marriage get married married couple couple divorce	associated expressions relationships in which marriage is not a factor partner partnership couple

3
1 F
2 E
3 G
4 B
5 C
6 A
7 D

4
1 T
2 F
3 F
4 T
5 NG
6 T
7 T
8 NG

5
1 compared to
2 between, rise
3 fewer
4 down from
5 risen

Reading Passage 6 p. 39

Multiple-choice questions p. 39

1 C
2 D
3 A
4 B
5 A

Completing sentences p. 41

6 online ads
7 revenues and profits
8 internet
9 websites

Identifying the writer's point of view p. 41

10 YES
11 NOT GIVEN
12 NO

13 YES
14 A ii
15 B i

Reading Passage 7 p. 42

Skills development p. 42

Verbs with modifiers:
i   may feel
ii   should not surprise
iii may have changed
iv   may have produced

i   D
ii   C
iii A
iv   B

True/False/Not given questions p. 42

1 FALSE. Section B – Homo sapiens *appeared about 3 million years ago.*
2 TRUE. Section A – *protected by tents of animal skins*
3 NOT GIVEN. There is no mention of caves, nor of what humans lived in before making tents, anywhere in the passage.
4 TRUE. Section B – *we who have witnessed the incredible changes brought to our cultures by the Industrial Revolution may feel that architecture has not changed much, at least over the last 6,000 years.*
5 NOT GIVEN. Section C – *tenements in … Rome had risen as high as ten stories* but we have no information about whether there were taller buildings.

Summary completion p. 44

A 4
B 5
C 6
D 1

Questions 6–10
6   architecture (Section B)
7   the weather (Section B)
8   defend (Section C)
9   exchange (Section C)
10 buildings (Section C)

Pictures and diagrams p. 45

1 D
2 C
3 E
4 F
5 A
6 B

Reading Passage 8 p. 45

1 TRUE. Section A, l.3 – *the technology crash notwithstanding*
2 FALSE. Section B, l.6 – *30% of American companies had identified rogue access-points*
3 FALSE. Section B, l.25 – *attract unwanted visitors*
4 FALSE. Section D, l.8 – *Anti-virus and firewall software exists for handheld computers*
5 TRUE. Section F, l.18 – *an 'inclusive' model that lays down who can do what, and only lets certain people do certain things*
6 NOT GIVEN. Hackers are not mentioned in the passage.
7 B

8 YES. Section B, l.25 – *by opening its systems to outsiders, a company may also attract unwanted visitors, or attacks from nosy competitors*

9 YES. Section D, l.7 – *improbably, a joint initiative by rivals Microsoft and IBM*

10 NO. Section B, l.1 – *Adding an access-point to a network costs less than $200 and is very simple*

11 NOT GIVEN.

12 present their credentials

13 employees/only employees

14 C

15 A

16 B

17 D/ E

18 1999

19 5 m (million)

20 2003

Key for Writing module

Quiz p. 48

1 B 60 minutes

2 A 20 minutes for Task 1 and 40 minutes for Task 2

3 B No. Because there are more marks for Task 2 – so it's important to give Task 2 no less than 40 minutes. You can learn to do Task 1 in 20 minutes if you write enough practice answers.

4 A Minimum 150 words for Task 1 and 250 words for Task 2

5 A Describing a diagram. This may contain statistical information, or show a process, a procedure or possibly a map.

6 B An essay discussing an issue of general interest

Writing Task 1 p. 48

Skills development p. 48

Understanding the task p. 48

Figure 1 How granulated sugar is produced

Figure 2 Life expectancy in the UK: Change over time

Figure 3 Percentage of the population who can speak a second language: Proportions

Figure 4 Attendance at Cultural Events in Great Britain: Change over time

Figure 5 Numbers of various types of restaurants in the city of Gastronome: Proportions

Figure 6 Adults accessing the internet in the UK: Change over time

Talking about the chart p. 50

1

1 What proportion of British adults used the internet in 2004. Figure 6

2 How many people go to see plays in the theatre. Figure 4.

3 How long men and women lived, on average, in 1981. Figure 2.

4 The percentage of people in Country E who can speak two languages. Figure 3.

5 The number of Chinese restaurants in Gastronome. Figure 5.

6 Sugar production. Figure 1.

2 and **3**

Figure 1 How granulated sugar is produced
  • This is a flow chart/a chart/a diagram/a figure.
  • It has a number of stages or steps.

Figure 2 Life expectancy in the UK
  • This is a chart/a graph/a line graph.
  • The horizontal axis shows life expectancy in years and the vertical axis shows time in 20-year intervals.
  • Note: the word *projections* means that the figures to the right of the dotted line are estimates – not true figures – because they are in the future.

Figure 3 Percentage of the population in six countries who can speak a second language
  • This is a chart/a graph/a bar chart.
  • The horizontal axis shows percentages (of the population who can speak a second language) and the vertical axis shows the six countries.
  • Remember in your answer to talk about the *proportion* or *percentage of people* – not *how many* people.

Figure 4 Attendance at Cultural Events in Great Britain
  • This is a table. It has rows (horizontal) and columns (vertical). It has no axes.
  • The rows show various *categories* (different *types* of events, eg cinema-going) and the columns show years (eg 2001–2).

Figure 5 Numbers of various type of restaurants in the city of Gastronome
  • This is a pie chart/a chart/a figure. It has segments and no axes.
  • The various segments represent different types of restaurants – specifically, how many there are of each type.

Figure 6 Adults accessing the internet in the UK
  • This is a bar chart/a chart.
  • The horizontal axis shows months and years and the vertical axis shows percentages of adults accessing the internet.

Reading the chart p. 50

1 It is filtered.

2 Approximately 68 and 75. It's only approximately because you're reading the figures from a graph which doesn't show very much detail.

3 About 36%.

4 Country C – about 58%.

5 A third (or one third).

6 Chinese, Indian and Italian.

7 Going to the cinema. We also call this cinema-going and the people who do it are called cinema-goers.

8 Classical music. Twelve per cent of British people – concert-goers – went to this kind of event.

9 Contemporary dance, varying between 3% and 5%.

10 Country F (about 4%).

11 Just under 60%.

12 (Sugar) crystals form.

Selecting the main features p. 51

1

1 • Life expectancy in the UK from 1901 to about 2025
  • The figures from about 2001 onwards are projections.
  • All figures are approximate.

2 • General trend is upward
    • Except very minor fluctuations in eg 1905, 1950 and 1970
    • More fluctuation than usual in 1930s

- Women higher than men – the gap is generally about 5 years (except c. 1918)
- Major drops in approximately 1914–18 and approximately 1940–42
3
- Growth rate generally a bit slower from about 1955 onwards
- Male/female gap increased 1950s and 60s (say eight years) then narrowed again
4
- Male/female gap (already mentioned)
- Amount of increase:
  - Women: 1901=48; 2002=81 (Projection for 2025=85)
  - Men: 1901=44; 2002=76 (Projection for 2025=81)

2

1
- The proportions of British adults accessing (using) the internet.
- The figures are at annual intervals (although the 2001 figure is for January and the others are for February of each year).
- The figures are percentages (not fractions or absolute numbers).
- All figures are approximate (because we have to read them from a chart).
- Again, we can see approximate proportions from the bar sizes, so this helps us to see comparisons.
2
- The chart shows fairly steady growth.
- There are no drops.
- The number of people using the internet rose by about 17–18% over five years
- … from under half (about 45% in January 2001)
- … to almost two-thirds (about 63% in February 2006).
- The rate of growth slowed a little in 2003–2005.
3
- There are no exceptions to the trend which shows a steady growth from January 2001 to February 2006.
- The rate of growth is slower between February 2004 and 2005 but picks up again from February 2005 and 2006.
4
- Amount of increase:
  - The rate of increase was greater between 2001–03 (8–9%) than between 2004–06 (4–5%).

Writing an introduction p. 51

Introductions 1: The topic

1

Sample answers:
In each case, compare the answer with the wording of the question. Note that these are only sample answers – there are of course other possibilities.

2

1 The bar chart illustrates the rates of children born underweight in seven global regions.
2 The figure gives information about the percentages of British people who attended various types of cultural events at five-year intervals from 1986–7 to 2001–2.
3 The pie chart is about children who are below average weight in the first five years of life. It shows numbers of such children in seven global regions.
4 The bar chart gives information about the money spent by people in the UK on magazines, newspapers and books.
5 The pie chart shows how mobile phone owners were distributed between six different parts of the world in 2006. The figures are percentages of the global total.
6 The table illustrates how people over 16 in the UK are occupied at various times of the day and night from Monday to Friday.

7 The data illustrates the changes that took place in population figures in the 50 years from 1950. Information is given for the world as a whole and for regions. There are also figures about the number of people living in cities and the expected growth to 2050.
8 The bar chart gives information based on police figures about serious crimes in a number of EU countries in the four years to 2000. It shows percentage changes for each country.
9 The diagram illustrates the main steps in the process by which chocolate is made.

Introductions 2: An overview

1 Figure 3
There are remarkable variations in the proportion of people who speak another language and only one country where the majority do.
2 Figure 4
With one exception, it shows remarkable consistency in attendance at the various kinds of event.
3 Figure 5
Three types of cuisine dominate the market.
4 Figure 6
It shows steady growth in the number of people using the internet.

Skills development p. 52

Tasks focusing on proportion p. 52

Language focus: Comparisons and numbers p. 52

1

Possible answers:
1 than
2 as, as
3 more, than
4 less
5 as
6 than
7 more

2

1 Russia has the biggest population.
2 There are more people in Russia than Oman.
3 Germany has a (much) bigger population than Canada.
4 Liberia has a (slightly) smaller population than Oman.
5 Liberia's population is almost the same as Oman's.
6 Canada's population is about ten times the size of Oman's.
7 Canada's population is about ten times as big as Oman's.
8 Russia's population is about twice as big as Germany's.
9 Russia's population is about twice the size of Germany's.

Language focus: Proportions p. 53

1

1 than in
2 almost twice
3 more than twice as
4 More than half
5 ten times as
6 Just under
7 the most
8 the second most
9 the least

2

Sample sentences:

Australia's population is only a third the size of France's population.

There are about three times as many people in France as in Australia.

At just over 60m, France's population is slightly larger than Italy's (about 58m).

Sudan's population is just over twice as big as Australia's.

Australia's population is just under half Sudan's. (Or: Australia's population is just under half *that of* Sudan.)

France has almost exactly three times Australia's population.

Planning your answer p. 54

Commentary

1 The key points are:
- The enormous change in cinema attendance
- Little or no change in all other categories

These need to be included in the overview. Effectively, there is no other information to be given (although the total lack of change in classical music attendance is an interesting detail).

2 But (Step 2) these two points need explaining and some detail must be given. It makes sense to give one paragraph to each of those two key points.

3 The sample answer is very good and meets all of the requirements in the *Checklist for a good answer.*

Skills practice

This has been prepared as an example of a very good answer. It is of course not the only way to answer the question well.

The pie chart illustrates the career choices of Bluesky University's 2006 graduates, giving the percentages who worked in each of various sectors after finishing university. Overwhelmingly, industry and government were the most popular choices.

Just under half the students went into industry, with service industries attracting more Bluesky graduates than any other sector by far – almost a third (33.0%). About half that number (16.3%) took jobs in manufacturing.

Politics and public service were the next most popular choice, accounting for nearly a fifth of graduates. Just over 12% went into politics and a further 5.6% chose the civil service.

The other significant career choices were education (about 15%) and two others: the arts, entertainment and media, with 7.8%; and science and technology with 7.3%.

The least popular choices included work in the charitable sector and careers in sport, both of which were chosen by well under 1% of graduates. Finally, 2.8% entered work in other, unspecified, sectors.

(157 words)

> **Remember**
> Some questions give you less material than others. Even if there is not very much data and it is hard to produce a 150-word answer, make sure you follow the Checklist on page 55. Organize your answer and do not simply list all the data.

Skills development p. 56

Tasks focusing on change over time p. 56

Proportional change p. 56

1
1 Visitors from overseas doubled.
2 UK residents making trips abroad tripled.

2
Sample answer:

The chart shows the number of trips abroad made by UK residents, and by overseas residents visiting the United Kingdom, from 1984 to 2004. Despite some variations, the most notable feature is an overall growth in both, although the number of visits abroad made by British people was considerably higher than the number of visits to the UK, and grew more rapidly.

Looking first at visits overseas by people in Britain, there was only one slight drop, in the mid-80s. There were also two periods with little or no growth, from the late 80s to early 90s, and again in the mid-90s. These are exceptions, though: otherwise the graph shows strong increases, from about 22 million visits in 1984 to about 64 million in 2004.

As for visits to Britain, these stood in 1984 at about 13 million and more than doubled to about 28 million in 2004. There was a significant drop around the beginning of the new century, followed by the strongest rise for some years.

(169 words)

3

Underlined text = information not shown on chart

Highlighted text = information shown on chart but impossible to see accurately on it

In 2004 overseas residents made a record 27.8 million visits to the UK and spent a record £13 billion. Taking inflation into account spending by overseas residents increased by 13 per cent between 1984 and 2004, and 7 per cent between 2003 and 2004.

The number of visits to the UK doubled between 1984 and 2004, with levels exceeding the previous high in 1998. Between 2003 and 2004 there was a 16 per cent increase in the number of holiday visits to the UK by overseas residents. This followed a decline of 18 per cent between 2000 and 2001, and only small recoveries in each of the following two years.

Residents of the USA made the largest number of visits to the UK – 3.6 million in 2004. French residents made 3.3 million visits, followed by residents of Germany (3.0 million visits), Ireland (2.6 million) and the Netherlands (1.6 million).

The number of visits abroad made by UK residents has almost tripled since 1984, to a record 64.2 million visits in 2004. Two-thirds of these visits abroad were holidays, just under half of which were package holidays. Although the number of holidays overall has continued to increase year-on-year, there has been little change in the number of package holidays in the last five years.

Europe remained the most popular destination for UK residents, accounting for over 80 per cent of visits abroad. Spain continued to be the most popular country to visit, with 13.8 million visits in 2004. France was second in popularity, with 11.6 million visits. The number of visits by UK residents to the USA increased by 15 per cent in 2004 to 4.2 million, although this was still 4 per cent lower than the number in 2000.

Spending on visits abroad by UK residents increased to a record £30.3 billion, a fourfold increase between 1984 and 2004 in real terms, and a 10 per cent increase between 2003 and 2004.

4

Underlined text = language used to present data

Highlighted text = language used to show relationships between figures, especially proportions (also ranking)

In 2004 overseas residents made a record 27.8 million visits to the UK and spent a record £13 billion. Taking inflation into account spending by overseas residents increased by 13 per cent between 1984 and 2004, and 7 per cent between 2003 and 2004.

The number of visits to the UK doubled between 1984 and 2004, with levels exceeding the previous high in 1998. Between 2003 and 2004 there was a 16 per cent increase in the number of holiday visits to the UK by overseas residents. This followed a decline of 18 per cent between 2000 and 2001, and only small recoveries in each of the following two years.

Residents of the USA made the largest number of visits to the UK – 3.6 million in 2004. French residents made 3.3 million visits, followed by residents of Germany (3.0 million visits), Ireland (2.6 million) and the Netherlands (1.6 million).

The number of visits abroad made by UK residents has almost tripled since 1984, to a record 64.2 million visits in 2004. Two-thirds of these visits abroad were holidays, just under half of which were package holidays. Although the number of holidays overall has continued to increase year-on-year, there has been little change in the number of package holidays in the last five years.

Europe remained the most popular destination for UK residents, accounting for over 80 per cent of visits abroad. Spain continued to be the most popular country to visit, with 13.8 million visits in 2004. France was second in popularity, with 11.6 million visits. The number of visits by UK residents to the USA increased by 15 per cent in 2004 to 4.2 million, although this was still 4 per cent lower than the number in 2000.

Spending on visits abroad by UK residents increased to a record £30.3 billion, a fourfold increase between 1984 and 2004 in real terms, and a 10 per cent increase between 2003 and 2004.

Verbs and nouns of change p. 58

1

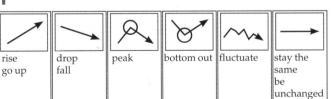

| rise go up | drop fall | peak | bottom out | fluctuate | stay the same be unchanged |

2

Verb	Noun
rise	a rise
go up	
increase	an increase
fall	a fall
drop	a drop
decrease	a decrease
peak	a peak
bottom out	
fluctuate	a fluctuation
be unchanged	
stay the same	

3

1 *Possible answers include:* rose/increased/went up
2 of
3 at
4 peaked
5 in
6 by
7 of

Expressing contrast p. 59

Possible answers:

1 There was a steady rise in the number of adults accessing the internet. In contrast, the percentage of households with an internet connection was rather lower.
2 Although there was a gradual increase in the percentage of homes with an internet connection, the relative popularity of broadband and narrowband changed radically.
3 Despite its use in about 40% of homes in April 2003, narrowband soon lost its popularity to broadband.
4 In spite of radical changes in the respective use of the two types of connection, the increase the overall number of connections was much less dramatic.

Planning your answer p. 59

1 Step 1: Analyse the data

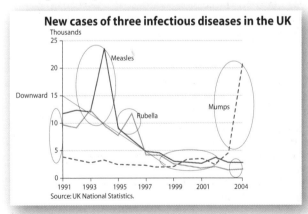

New cases of three infectious diseases in the UK

Main features (in no particular order):
Large variations – outbreaks of all 3 diseases at different times
Mumps by far the lowest (2 000–4 000) till 1999
Measles and rubella: overall fall despite outbreaks (peaks: measles 23 000 in 1994, rubella 12 000 in 1996) – then remarkable falls

All 3 at low levels 1999–2002
Then mumps rises, first rapidly, then very rapidly, to 21 000

Comparisons:
Measles and rubella (some close similarities) compared with mumps (mostly very different)
Probably a good idea to give 1991 levels, so the reader has a comparison for all other figures
Also compare 2004 figures

2 Step 2: Organize your material

1
Commentary
Approach 1: Say what happened in each year from 1991 to 2004.
This is not recommended. It will involve a lot of detail and probably too many figures. The main features will be hard to highlight and will get lost in the detail. You will not have space to make comparisons. The result will not be a summary and it will be hard work for the reader to pick out the main features from your answer. You are likely to run out of time.
Approach 2: Talk about each disease separately.
This would give three paragraphs in the main body of your answer, one for each disease. It will be easier to follow than Approach 1, but you will still have difficulty providing a summary rather than a mass of detail.
Approach 3: Talk about the main features you identified.
This is recommended because it will be easier to do what the task demands: summarize the information by selecting and reporting the main features and make comparisons where relevant.

2
Notes for a possible plan
1   Introduction. What the data is about. The most obvious feature: despite large variations – outbreaks of all 3 diseases at different times – general falls until sudden mumps outbreak.
2   Measles and rubella: overall fall despite outbreaks (peaks: measles 23 000 in 1994, rubella 12 000 in 1996) – then remarkable falls. Note similarities, eg 1997–2004.
3   Contrast: mumps by far the lowest (2 000–4 000) till 1999. All 3 at low levels 1999–2002.
4   Then mumps rose, first rapidly, then very rapidly, to 21 000. (4 000 in 1991). Compare measles and rubella 2004 figures with 1991 levels.

3 Writing up your answer

Highlighted text = language for linking

The graph gives approximate figures for UK measles, mumps and rubella infections between 1991 and 2004. Despite large variations, it shows a general fall until a sudden increase in mumps in the last two years.

Cases of measles and rubella tended to fall, although there were sudden rises in both, causing peaks of 23 000 for measles in 1994 and 12 000 for rubella two years later. Both then showed remarkable falls and followed very similar trends from 1997 to 2004, with the rate of measles infections being generally a little higher.

In contrast, mumps cases fluctuated between 2 000 and 4 000 until 1999 and, although they began to rise a little, all three diseases had very low rates (below 4 000) until 2002.

At this point the figures for mumps began to rise, first rapidly and then more so, to reach 21 000 in 2004, with no indication of a slowdown – compared with a level of 4 000 in 1991. The corresponding figures for measles were a fall from 12 000 cases in 1991 to 3 000 in 2004; and for rubella, from 10 000 to 2 000.

Combined tasks p. 60

Sample answer:
The charts illustrate the changing patterns of internet use among adults in the UK in January 2001 and in the February of the following five years; and the changes in household internet connections between April 2003 and July 2005. Two aspects of the data are particularly striking: first, that people steadily used the web more and more; and second, that broadband replaced narrowband as the most popular type of connection.

From January 2001 to February 2006, the proportion of adults accessing the internet rose from about 46% to about 62%. The rate of increase was rapid over the first two years, fell a little in 2004, and accelerated again in 2005.

In the two years from April 2003 there was a less steady increase in the proportion of households with an internet connection, of about 6%, to about 56%. The most interesting trend, despite some fluctuations, was the steady fall in the popularity of narrowband connections (from about 40% about 25%) and the corresponding increase in the use of broadband (from about 8% to about 32%).

(176 words)

Skills practice p. 61

Note: there is not very much to report here in the way of trends and exceptions. You need to be careful that you do not simply write a description of all the data – and that you present a clear, strong overview in the introduction.

Sample answer:
The chart illustrates the changing trends in smoking among the UK population, by sex, for a period of about 30 years from 1974 onwards. The most obvious change was a general fall in the proportion of both men and women who smoked – by almost exactly half, in the case of men, and by a little less in the case of women.

The proportion of male smokers stood at about 52% in 1974. It then fell, with variations in the rate of fall, to around 30% in about 1994, when it began to rise again, peaking in 1998–9, when it began to fall once more. There was another slight rise in about 2004 before the downward trend continued, ending at about 26% in 2004–5.

The pattern among the female population was broadly similar, with an overall fall from about 42% in 1974 to about 24% at the end of the period. There was only one slight rise, between 1994–5 and 1996–7.

(159 words)

Skills development p. 62

Tasks focusing on processes p. 62

Planning your answer p. 62

Sample answer:
The flowchart shows the main stages in the recycling of glass drinks bottles.

In the first stage recycled glass, soda ash, sand and other raw materials are fed into a furnace where they are heated to 1500° C and melted. From here they pass to the fore hearth, where the temperature is homogenized. The next stage is the cutting machine, which cuts the molten glass into identical pieces.

In the forming machine the molten glass pieces are forced into moulds, producing the bottle shape. They are cooled to below 1150° before passing to the rapid cooling stage, in which the temperature falls to below 500°. The next stage is conditioning, where the bottles are warmed again to 1200° before being cooled to under 500°, which strengthens them. They are then ready for surface treatment, which involves first cooling the bottles to 120° before spraying to provide a smooth finish.

Quality checks identify faults and any rejects are recycled in the furnace, while the finished bottles are packed.

(167 words)

Writing your answer p. 63

Active or passive? p. 63

1

Underlined text = passive verbs

Highlighted text = active verbs

The flowchart shows the main stages in the recycling of glass drinks bottles.

In the first stage recycled glass, soda ash, sand and other raw materials are fed into a furnace where they are heated to 1500° C and melted. From here they pass to the fore hearth, where the temperature is homogenised. The next stage is the cutting machine, which cuts the molten glass into identical pieces.

In the forming machine the molten glass pieces are forced into moulds, producing the bottle shape. They are cooled to below 1150° before passing to the rapid cooling stage, in which the temperature falls to below 500°. The next stage is conditioning, where the bottles are warmed again to 1200° before being cooled to under 500°, which strengthens them. They are then ready for surface treatment, which involves first cooling the bottles to 120° before spraying to provide a smooth finish.

Quality checks identify faults and any rejects are recycled in the furnace, while the finished bottles are packed.

2

1 a The liquids are mixed in a mixing chamber.
2 a The director chooses his team. (The director is important because he/she is the leader, the person who makes the decision.)
3 b The water is heated. (It is very strange – and adds no information – to say that people do this. The focus is on the event, the action, not on who performs it.)
4 a The mixture is boiled. (Again, it is strange to say that technicians do this. The focus is on the event, the action, not on who performs it.)
5 a The gas passes along the pipe.
   b The gas is passed along the pipe.
Both forms are acceptable.
6 a The mixture passes through a filter.
   b The mixture is filtered.
Both forms are acceptable.
7 b The mixture passes through a filter, which removes impurities.
8 b The product is tested.
   c The product undergoes testing.
Undergo + -ing form is an alternative to the passive when we talk about production processes.
9 b The product is irradiated to kill germs.
   c The product undergoes irradiation to kill germs.

Describing stages p. 64

1 First
2 here
3 through/via (*along* is not possible because it's a membrane, not a pipe)
4 into/to
5 where/in which
6 After that/Next
7 into (because it is a container)
8 a further stage/step
9 through/via/along (*along* is possible here because it is a pipe)

Writing Task 2 p. 65

Quiz p. 65

1 True.
2 Yes, you can, but it's a bad idea. There are more marks for Task 2 so, if you are short of time, give less to Task 1.
3 False. You need to write 250 words or more.
4 True. In fact the question tells you that you must give reasons for your answer.
5 True. You may miss the main point of the question if you do not.
6 False. This is usually a serious mistake. Take time to plan and make sure you answer the question directly.
7 False. You need to write a minimum of 250 words.
8 If this is the only way you can give 40 minutes to Task 2, yes. But a better approach may be to read the Task 2 question before answering Task 1. While you are doing Task 1, you will be thinking, unconsciously, about ideas for Task 2.

Skills development p. 65

Understanding the task p. 65

1

1 C
2 A
3 B
4 A
5 A
6 B

Planning 1: Brainstorming p. 67

1

The question is Type B. You need to look at different viewpoints as well as your own and come to a conclusion. (You need to say where you think the balance is between differing points of view. It is not enough simply to say that people disagree.) Some questions contain two parts – that is, two issues you have to write about – but this one does not.

2

Possible ideas:

Reasons for privacy	Reasons against privacy
Individuals' rights	Public's rights
Pain as entertainment = wrong	Celebrities can't choose when they want publicity
Media want money or morality?	Fun
Leaders need to feel trusted	Expose liars
Focus media on big issues, not scandal	

These ideas are not the only ones – and perhaps not even the best ones.

Notice how short these notes are. In fact they can be shorter if the writer is only person who needs to understand them.

3

The task is Type A. You need to explain your views and come to a conclusion.
Possible ideas:

Agree	Disagree
It works (safety)	Reform
Punishment	Prison = training for criminals
Revenge	Expensive
Deterrence	Should have to work
	Not a very nice place

Deterrence means 'the idea that people will decide not to do something if they believe that something unpleasant could happen to them as a result'. (*Macmillan English Dictionary*).

Reform means 'a change in someone's behaviour so that it is no longer illegal or harmful'. (*Macmillan English Dictionary*).

Planning 2: Selecting ideas and evidence p. 67

1

Agree

Individuals' rights – A good strong, point on moral grounds
Pain as entertainment = wrong – Again, a good moral point
Media want money or morality? – And another
Leaders need to feel trusted – If the job of the leaders is to make the country a good place for the people, then arguably they will do a better job if they feel their mistakes may be exposed. The point is not logical.
Focus media on big issues, not scandal – You could argue this point either way. (a) Yes, diverting the media away from scandal to more serious issues might be a good thing but (b) the media manage to do both these things anyway. So this is not the strongest point and is secondary to the moral ones.

Disagree

Public's rights – Yes, the public have a right to know when their leaders mislead or lie to them. But is it also true that we have the right to know intimate details of politicians' – and celebrities' – lives?
Celebrities can't choose when they want publicity – You could argue that celebrities profit from publicity and therefore must be ready to suffer from it as well. But if you argue that individuals have a moral right to privacy, then this point looks much weaker.
Fun – People do sometimes enjoy seeing others' misfortunes publicized but this is not a very noble motivation. More seriously, this point is about pleasure, while some of the others are about moral rights and principles of good government. This point is very weak in comparison.
Expose liars – This is a very important point if we are talking about leaders and politicians (perhaps less so if we are only talking about sports and pop stars).

2

Agree

It works (safety) – There are many people who will commit further serious crimes if released, eg some murderers. The only way to stop them offending again is by locking them up. It's difficult to argue against this point unless you argue that they should be executed instead – but remember that 'serious crimes' include many things, not just murder, so you may be arguing that quite a wide range of criminals should be executed, and you may find this hard to justify.
Punishment – You could argue that this is the real point of locking people up in prison – but it's not really relevant. The point is: should we keep such people in prison for as long as possible to ensure that they cannot commit more crimes?
Revenge – You could argue that this is important– but it's not relevant. The point is: should we keep such people in prison for as long as possible to ensure that they cannot commit more crimes?
Deterrence – Again, this is not really relevant. But if you argue that prison works, then this could make a good secondary point: just don't give it much space.

Disagree

Reform – You could argue that we should reform criminals, not just lock them up, so that long sentences are not appropriate. But then you will need to show that reform programmes do prevent people from committing serious crimes again (this is true in some cases but not in all).
Prison = training for criminals – In other words, it makes no sense to put criminals there because they will only get worse. But people who have already committed serious crimes are already capable of doing so and may need no help in learning

to commit more – so this point is not strong unless you can show that prison teaches serious criminals how to commit more crimes without getting caught.

Expensive – This is a strong argument. It will not help you support the idea of reform though, unless you can show that reform is more effective than prison in preventing serious criminals from re-offending. You could use it to support the idea of executing people who commit serious crimes, but again remember that 'serious crime' covers a wide range.

Should have to work – Not relevant because prisons can arrange for prisoners to make money by working in prison, thus supporting the prison system financially.

Prison is not a very nice place – Again, not relevant.

3

Possible answers:

2   People become interested in their personal lives – their friendships, relationships, family life and so on. This is what creates the public interest which makes people famous – and of course rich – in the first place.
3   If people do not have enough food, in fact enough of the right food, then they become ill through lack of basic physical needs, such as proteins and vitamins.

4

Possible answers:

1   In addition to providing food, clothing and other necessities for prisoners, the service also needs to pay staff and pay for expensive security arrangements.
2   It may not be able to reform many criminals, but it does keep them in a secure environment where they are unable to repeat their crimes. Many murderers and other serious crimes are prevented in this way.
3   They may have no experience at all of a normal job, for example, no qualifications, and no hope of ever finding a job. Also, after some years in prison their closest friends may be other criminals and other relationships may not be as strong as they once were.
4   In prison they cannot gain any experience of normal working life, or any of the skills they would need in employment. On the other hand, they are likely to be influenced by other criminals and to learn more criminal skills from them.
5   In many countries, tobacco is heavily taxed so that the price the smoker pays is many times more than the price the tobacco company charges.

Planning 3: Deciding your viewpoint p. 68

1

This answer has many plus points, but one main weakness: the writer did not think out his point of view before he started writing. Instead, he thought through the issues while writing. As a result the viewpoint expressed in the introduction is quite different from the conclusion. This seriously weakens his answer. With a little more thought it could have been more impressive.

Planning 4: Planning your answer p. 69

1

1   This plan has no introduction. As a result it will be harder for the reader to follow the argument.
2   This plan does not talk about possible measures to reduce the problems. This is a serious lack: the answer is ignoring half the question.

3   This plan follows a logical order but puts the whole of the main body into one extremely long paragraph. This is poor organization since it makes it much harder for the reader to follow the progression of topics and ideas.
4   This plan does not talk about causes of the problem. This is a serious lack: the answer is ignoring half the question.
5   This is not a logical order. It makes no sense to talk about how to solve the problem before talking about what the causes are.
6   This is a sensible, logical plan. The paragraphs will each follow on logically from the last. As a result it will be easier to write and the reader will follow the progression of topics and ideas more easily.

2

Paragraph 1	Introduction: Exams are not perfect but are a necessity
Paragraph 2	Disadvantages of exams
Paragraph 3	Advantages of exams
Paragraph 4	Improvements possible by mixing exams with other systems (eg long-term assessment)
Paragraph 5	Conclusion: This is probably the best balance which can be achieved; and often traditional exams are the only possibility

Planning 5: Checking your plan p. 70

1   This candidate probably wrote about the general topic but didn't think carefully about the question – and so wrote an answer which was not a direct answer. The essay was probably not very relevant to the question.
2   The same comment applies – and this candidate did not plan an answer. As a result the answer was probably badly organized and only partly relevant.
3   For the same reasons, this candidate is not likely to achieve his or her maximum potential result in the exam. Another danger of not planning is that you are more likely to leave your answer unfinished after 40 minutes.

Skills development 2 p. 71

Writing your answer p. 71

The introduction p. 71

1   This simply repeats the question and says the writer does not know the answer (but then goes on to suggest one cause). However, the question asks you to list causes and possible solutions so you need to do so. This is a weak introduction and gives us no idea what to expect in the main body of the answer except confusion and a lack of ideas.
2   This is not a promising introduction. It gives us no clue as to the writer's point of view and (if a few words were changed) could be used as the first paragraph for more or less any Type A or B question, which indicates how irrelevant it is. The writer is more interested in repeating some familiar phrases than in answering the question. Also, at 65 words, it is a quarter of the minimum 250: in fact, this paragraph is a waste of 25% of the candidate's answer.
3   This paragraph is well-written and reasonably interesting but, offers no indication of the writer's viewpoint. We have the feeling that the answer has not really started yet but 25% of the minimum word limit has already been used.

4   This is a direct answer to the question asked. We do not yet know why the writer thinks what he/she does: but we know his/her point of view and we can confidently expect that the main body will explain the reasons for this view.

5   This longer version of No. 3 is clearer because it goes on to suggest (but not yet explain) what the writer's view is. However, it is very long for Task 2 (46% of 250 words) and the main body of the essay has not yet begun. Also, the writer will now need to go back to the ideas already touched on in the first paragraph and explain them more fully, which will take time and many words. It is a good introduction for a much longer essay than IELTS – perhaps a 1000-word answer.

Skills practice p. 72

1

Sample introductions:

1   The lack of food is one of the most serious problems facing the world today, causing malnutrition and starvation for millions of human beings. However, this situation can be solved by organized and determined international efforts.

2   Malnutrition and starvation affect millions of human beings. The tragedy of this situation is that it could be solved if the international community were prepared to address it in an organized and determined way.

3   Almost a billion people around the world today are hungry. The tragedy of this situation is that it could be solved if the international community were prepared to address it in an organized and determined way.

All of these are reasonable introductory paragraphs. The word 'tragedy' in 2 and 3 make the writer's feelings clear, whereas they are not obvious in 1. 3 is an example of how a stark fact can add strength to your argument, and gain attention, without including much information, but of course this approach is not suitable for all questions. Notice that there is not much information in any of these because most of the information will be in the main body, supporting the arguments there.

Skills development p. 72

The main body p. 72

1

1   False. One paragraph = one main topic. There may be a number of examples within the paragraph.

2   False. You need to plan the whole essay before you start writing. This means you need to know how many paragraphs you will write and what the topic of each one will be. You also need to know what information, ideas and examples you will use within the paragraph.

3   False. Quality, not quantity. You will probably not have time in less than 35 minutes (5 for planning, remember, and a few minutes for checking your answer) to write about more than 3 or 4 main ideas. Essays with a large number of paragraphs are usually poorly organized and therefore confusing.

4   False. The important thing is to explain what you mean clearly. If your English level is very high then you probably will use some impressive language. If your level is lower, focus on trying to communicate clearly and effectively. Remember, the examiner can see the overall level of your English and will not be impressed by a few special phrases thrown in to look good.

5   True. This means that you have thought about the task and planned your answer.

2

The ideas fall into four groups:
Population
High population
Economics
Growing gap between rich and poor
Unfair trading practices
Aid
Lack of money spent on relief and development
Wrong sort of aid
Corruption in poor countries: aid goes to the wrong people
Climate change

3

Population
High population **and** rapid population growth
Economics
Growing gap between rich and poor: within nations and between them
Unfair trading practices, eg trade barriers which prevent poorer nations selling to richer ones at a fair price; big retailers (eg supermarket groups) forcing down suppliers' prices
Aid
Lack of money spent on relief and development
Wrong sort of aid, eg food: feeds people for a short time but doesn't help them grow their own
Corruption in poor countries: aid goes to wrong people
Climate change
eg expanding deserts –> loss of fertile land
eg changing rainfall patterns –> floods, unpredictable harvests and loss of fertile land (eg in Bangladesh)

Note: There is probably too much material here for a Task 2 essay. We will probably have to reduce it a little.

4

The paragraph has a lot of good material but is no more than a list of sentences. It is not yet a good paragraph because there are no connections between the sentences: no glue to hold the ideas together, to make them into a whole. And there is no introductory or concluding sentence.

5

There are many ways to write these sentences. Here are suggested answers:
Introductory sentence: There are many reasons for the lack of food.
Concluding sentence: All this means there are millions who do not have enough to eat.

Notice how both these sentences refer directly to the question (*What do you think are some of the causes of this problem?*).

Language focus: Ordering ideas; linking cause and effect p. 73

There are many ways to do this. Here is a suggested answer:

There are many reasons for the lack of food. One is overpopulation, and the very high growth rate, which mean the world needs much, much more food. Secondly, our economic system is at fault: causing a growing gap between rich and poor; partly by preventing poorer nations from selling goods at a fair price. These problems are compounded by the lack of aid – aid which often does not address the underlying problems. <u>A final problem is</u> climate change, <u>which</u> reduces available farming land through expansion of deserts and through flooding. <u>All this means there are millions who do not have enough to eat.</u>

Notice how you can use a colon (:) like an arrow, pointing to a connected idea or example.

Skills practice p. 74

Suggested paragraph:
- Basic plan: at least one measure for each of the problems listed in paragraph 2.
- Notice the introductory and concluding sentences and, again, how both refer directly to the question (*What measures could be taken to reduce this problem?*).

<u>There is much we can do to address these problems.</u> <u>A major priority is</u> to slow the population growth, especially by giving developing countries resources for family planning services and public awareness campaigns. Rich countries need to rethink their use of resources, reduce waste and reform trading practices<u>:</u> the Fair Trade campaign is an example of this. <u>Another obvious measure is</u> debt cancellation for poor nations so that profits from trade can go to development rather than banks. <u>Finally,</u> on climate change, we have to stop burning fossil fuels. <u>All these are long-term projects, so we need to make a serious start on them now.</u>

Skills development p. 74

The conclusion p. 74

1

1 False. Say what you mean as clearly as you can. Do not worry about using special language to impress the examiner. The better your English is, the more creatively you can do it. If your English is not at that stage yet, then focus on communicating effectively, not on pretending your English is marvellous!
2 False. You should deal with your arguments in the main body.
3 False. The function of the conclusion is to remind the reader of your overall point of view.
4 True. The function of the conclusion is to remind people very clearly of the point of view which you started developing in the introduction, and to draw the essay to a close so the reader knows you have finished what you want to say.

2

Comments on conclusions
None of these is very good because:
1 This is too short and too informal. Even more importantly, it does not summarize the writer's viewpoint.
2 This is a great introduction – and in fact it is simply the introductory paragraph, copied out word for word. You don't need to say anything very different in the conclusion but you need to say it differently, reminding people of what has been said in the main body (whereas the introduction is a preview of the main body).
3 Although this says enough (summarizing the writer's viewpoint), it is too short. If you run out of time in the exam and have only a few seconds to write a conclusion, then this would be a good conclusion in the time available.

3

Possible conclusion:
The causes of world food shortages are complex and major work is needed to address them. In more than one case a major review of how we organize our world may be necessary – and massive, co-ordinated international action.

Skills practice p. 74

How to answer cause and effect questions p. 74

1

Possible ideas:

Right uses of money
- Improve lives – own family
- Develop children and adults – study and train
- Pleasure
- Culture: attending concerts and theatre, for example, or buying a musical instrument; emergencies and retirement
- Giving

Other factors important for a good life
- All elements above are important but:
- Good life = in relation to others
  - Family, community, work
  - Give and receive

2

Possible conclusion: Money not essential for good life but helps.

3

Sample answer:
Money has an important impact on most people's lives, whether by being plentiful or in short supply. While it cannot buy happiness, it can provide much that is of value.

In my view the right use of money is to improve people's lives, starting with one's own family. First, it helps to provide the means for people to develop themselves – by supporting children's growth, education and interests, through enabling adults to study and train or re-train and to develop skills to a high level. A third way in which money contributes is to provide pleasure, so that family members can pursue hobbies and enjoy holidays. Money is also necessary for many cultural interests: attending concerts and theatre, for example, or buying a musical instrument. A further use of money is to provide security against emergencies and in retirement. Last and not least, one of the right uses of money is to give to others, perhaps in the form of charity, so they can enjoy the same things that we can.

All the elements of life mentioned above are important, but ultimately people find satisfaction – a good life, that is – in relation to other humans. We need to be part of a community, to give and receive, to have relationships with others in family, community and work environments. We need to be useful and to help others. The contributions we can make (or receive) in these endeavours may or may not be financial.

In other words, money is not the only, or even the most important, factor in developing a good life, but it can certainly make an important contribution.

(269 words)

Checking your answer p. 77

2

Subject-verb agreement

To avoid repetition use 'several'

Too informal, use 'Many' — A lot of people <u>feels</u> this question have <u>many</u>

Singular/plural

Subject-verb agreement

different <u>answer</u>. Indeed, every coin <u>have</u> two

sides. In my country there is much debate about

this vexed issue and no agreement about the

Avoid use of cliché and memorized language

answer.

Repetition of 'good' in one sentence

Some people say <u>exam is good way</u> to find out

Singular/plural agreement and use of articles

Incorrect use of 'so'

who is <u>good</u> at a subject and who is not <u>so good</u>.

<u>They're right really in one way because if you</u>

Avoid use of contractions and questions. Better to state opinions.

<u>don't have exams, how can you find out who has</u>

<u>learned the necessary skills and information?</u>

People often forget that <u>the</u> knowledge is very

No article —

important, not just skills. There are many people

Incorrect word (use 'who') — <u>they</u> do not understand this. <u>Exam best way</u> to test

'Exams are the'

how much people know.

Too informal. Better to use 'In my opinion'

But is there a better way? <u>I think</u> nobody <u>have</u> a

Subject-verb agreement

system can work better. Except maybe continuous

Singular/plural —

assessment, when <u>teacher</u> give marks all the <u>year,</u>

Split long sentence into 2 shorter sentences.

<u>then</u> at the end of the year they add up all the

marks, this gives a score instead of the exam.

Conclusion is too short. Should be longer.

<u>In conclusion I can say there are many ways to test</u>

<u>what people learn.</u>

Key for Speaking module

Quiz p. 78

1 C
2 B
3 B
4

Part 1

1 False. 4-5 minutes
2 False. Fairly short answers, quite a lot of questions; a few sentences about each.
3 True. Topics may include your work, studies, family, home town, interests, hobbies, etc.

Part 2

4 True
5 False. You have to speak for 1–2 minutes on a topic the interviewer gives you.
6 False. During the Speaking test the interviewer will give you a topic to talk about and you will have 1 minute to prepare before you speak. It's important not to try to prepare a talk in advance.

Part 3

7 True
8 False. You won't get so many questions and this is a chance for you to give longer answers, developing your thoughts more.
9 False. You simply answer questions and discuss issues related to the topic you talked about in Part 2.

Part 1 p. 78

The topics you need to talk about p. 78

All are possible topics for Part 1 except:

- Your country's economic situation – not enough personal relevance to you
- i-pods – not enough personal relevance to you
- James Bond – again, probably no personal relevance to you (and you may know nothing about him)
- History – not enough personal relevance to you
- The Industrial Revolution – not enough personal relevance to you
- The price of oil and gas – not enough personal relevance to you
- Something very sad which has happened in your life – too personal

Possible questions p. 78

1 Your home town:
Do you come from a town, village or city?
Was it a nice place to grow up?
Can you describe it?
What is it best known for?
Is there anything you don't like about it?

2 Your work:
What kind of work do you do?
What do you enjoy about your work?
What don't you like about it?
Why did you choose that occupation?
What would you like to achieve in the future?

What makes a good answer p. 79

1 Comments

A ☺ This seems to be a memorized answer. It gives the interviewer no information about the speaker's English.
B ☺ Good answer. The most important thing is that it's relevant. It also shows a good variety of language.
C ☺ Again, a direct answer. It also deals well with the fact that the speaker has not lived in his home town for a long time and feels that it's no longer really his home.
D ☺ It's good to expand your answer, and anyone would sympathize with this candidate. He could talk about the fact that he is now hoping to work in this country, once qualified, in order to develop his already-established career; but his remarks could be seen as an attempt to influence the examiner.
E ☺ This answer is too short. It gives the examiner no language to assess.
F ☺ Some people panic if asked a question about a subject they're not interested in. This excellent response shows how you can handle such questions without pretending an interest you don't feel.

3 Re-writes

A I come from a city called Cadiz. That's on the south coast of Spain, on the Atlantic side. It's the provincial capital but in fact it's not a huge place – I'm not sure of the exact population, although I think it's round about 150,000 – so I suppose it's what you'd call a smallish city.
D I'm a doctor, although I'm in full-time study at the moment. I've built up a good practice at home and now I've come here for career development. Once I qualify to work in this country, I hope to be able to specialize in paediatrics and work in a leading unit. The right experience could lead to a consultancy back home and the chance to help a lot of people.
E See B.

Identifying strengths and weaknesses p. 80

1

Interview 1
The candidate is quite fluent and confident. She handles the questions very naturally. This helps give us the feeling that we have not yet begun to see how good her English is – and, of course, this is just the preparatory part before Part 1 begins.

Interview 2
He is a very strong candidate in terms of flexibility, fluency and language resource. All his language appears superbly natural and appropriate. His weakness is his accent. He needs to slow his speech down and take care to move his lips and tongue more than usual, like a theatre actor: this may seem a little strange, but will help him to communicate better; and one of the marking criteria for the Speaking test is of course Pronunciation.

Interview 3
He has a reasonable level of English but is not able to show it. He is nervous and this reduces his effectiveness – but his main problem is that he is not sure how best to handle the questions. He needs practice in answering questions like these before taking the Speaking test.

Interview 4

This candidate has responded to the problem of preparation we saw in Interview 3 by memorizing some answers which he hopes to give during the Speaking test. This is always a bad idea: candidates need to practise flexibility, not 'learned' answers. He is so keen to deliver one of his 'learned' answers that he gives this one at an inappropriate moment: the interviewer simply wants to know where he is from (Part 1 of the test has not even started). The candidate in Interview 1 showed us how to handle the same question in a much better way. His memory of his 'learned' answer is not perfect so it contains a number of mistakes.

Interview 5

This is a very strong candidate with an excellent range of language. She handles the questions spontaneously and very effectively. Notice how she deals with the first question, even though she does not have much free time. Because she did not panic, there is plenty to talk about in answer to the following questions too. She is relaxed enough to stop talking when she has answered each question, so the interviewer does not need to interrupt her at all.

Interview 6

Although he has a good basic level of fluency and knows enough vocabulary to talk about the topic, he makes a number of basic grammatical mistakes. More importantly, he does not organize his answer in any way: he simply says whatever comes into his mind. The interviewer cannot allow him to give very long answers because the maximum time for the Speaking test is only 14 minutes and Part 1 is of course no more than 5 minutes. As a result he will be interrupted often, with the topic changing each time, which will mean an uncomfortable, confusing Speaking test for him.

Part 2 p. 81

Planning your answer p. 81

1 Key words:
- letter – you received/wrote – important
- who to/from
- what – said
- what – special
- why – important – today

2 Key words:
- machine – important
- what
- how – got
- what – use – for
- why – important

3
- He says what it is and talks a lot about what he uses it for. He says a little about how he discussed buying it with his parents, although he doesn't say how he got it. The fact that it's important to him is clear from what he says but he doesn't explain why it's important to him.
- His language is reasonably correct, although he uses a fairly limited range of vocabulary and grammar structures:
  - He knows some current slang such as *cool* and *I mean, like I've …*
  - *I have some friends, we get a lot of these CDs*
  - *You can do a lot of … games*
- Some of what he says is a bit repetitive (eg *Maybe some of these friends are really friends, you know, like people you know in your studies or in your university, but also other friends who maybe I have never met in my life …*)

Identifying strengths and weaknesses p. 83

Candidate 1
She needs more material. She has covered all the questions but has not said enough about them. This means that she does not show much evidence of how good her English is so the examiner can only see this limited range. She could improve her performance by making sure she has 3 points or more for each question. For example, when talking about how the place made an impression on her she mentions only the names of some animals – perhaps she wrote the word 'animals' in her notes. Perhaps she could also have talked about 'feelings' and 'scenery'. This would remind her to talk about her impressions of the animals – that the emus were quite frightening in a way but that she felt more comfortable with them after feeding one – and to talk about the very dramatic scenery at the park.

Candidate 2
This is a very full answer: he covers all aspects of the question and speaks for around 3 minutes, which gives him the chance to show the range of language he can use. He knows some special vocabulary for talking about the cathedral – stained glass and so on – but more impressive is the non-technical language: for example,

- … *really one of the great buildings of Europe.*
- *It's a very special piece of architecture, so beautiful, with such fine lines, so tall.*
- *…something quite unexpected.*
- … *not so much because of what it looks like but because of how it makes you feel.*

This shows a good range of language as well as good fluency and organization. Although there are mistakes and some gaps in his vocabulary (*something quite unexpected for me happened, the formal part of the cathedral, impressing*) they do not seriously interfere with these positive qualities.

Candidate 3
He speaks fairly fluently, despite occasional hesitations and self-corrections, speaks for long enough, and covers all aspects of the question. On the other hand, what he says is not really organized and does not follow the order of topics in the instructions he was given. He uses a fair range of vocabulary and there are signs of one or two idiomatic expressions (*quite romantic, something like that*). His grammar is not very accurate and at times he corrects himself. Apart from overusing continuous tenses, he makes mistakes with more complex structures (*if I would have the same choice*).

Follow-up questions p. 84

Candidate 1
The candidate thinks the examiner wants him to continue demonstrating how good his English is (and we know he's able to talk at length!) but this particular question is only intended to end Part 2 so the examiner can then lead into Part 3. This is why the examiner interrupts.

Candidate 2
She needs to say more but isn't sure how to do it appropriately.

Candidate 3
This is an excellent answer. She says enough to answer the question appropriately and then stops.

Part 3 p. 84

Identifying strengths and weaknesses p. 85

Candidate 1

He talks about one general issue – that there is a lot of stress for young people today and he gives some examples and details which support his viewpoint. However, this is not the question he was asked. He has seen this question as an opportunity to repeat a statement which he has made before and perhaps prepared for the exam.

Candidate 2

She talks well about the question. She identifies one main abstract idea – that it depends where you live – and then uses plentiful detail to give her own country as an example – she then goes on to look briefly at a different case, without giving specifics (perhaps because she is being diplomatic about the interviewer's country). Although she could look at other general issues – serious social problems in some of the more comfortable countries she mentions, for example – her answer is certainly appropriate, relevant, thoughtful and long enough.

Candidate 3

At first he is not sure what the question is and asks for clarification. He gives his uncle as a concrete case and then gives plenty of detail. The contrast with his own situation makes the general point very convincingly and his point of view comes over clearly. Although he could look at other general issues – the changes in business and study methods, for example – he produces an appropriate answer which is certainly long enough.

Key for Practice test

Listening p. 87

1 Alnazri
2 195 Hills Road
3 07942 116470
4 CDs or DVDs/CDs, DVDs (both needed for a mark)
5 $1.50/One dollar fifty (*not* 1.50)
6 RBC 09 61 09
7 B – Main reading room
8 E – Canteen
9 D – Main computer suite
10 A – Toilets
11 C
12 B
13 B
14 A
15 A
16 seminar
17 computer laboratory
18 Open bank account.
19 informal meetings
20 Check newsletter.
21 C
22 B
23 B
24 A
25 A
26 B
27 motivation
28 exchange classes
29 books and magazines
30 listening

31 A
32 B
33 Bath
34 50°/50 degrees/Fifty degrees
35 eighteenth century/18th c./18th cent.
36 Switzerland
37 medicinal purposes
38 B
39 C
40 B

Reading p. 90

1 D
2 F
3 F
4 A
5 C
6 skills and aptitudes
7 motor and cognitive
8 technically literate
9 social
10 TRUE – Para A: 'The idea of bringing computer games in the classroom seems likely to provoke more detentions than learning. But that's slowly changing.'
11 FALSE – Para A: 'Gaming … is thought by many teachers and parents to be the classic sign of a modern wasted youth.'
12 FALSE – Para B: '… 60% believed they would … acquire specific knowledge.'
13 NOT GIVEN
14 E – Para 3: 'The study found … which demonstrates neither altruism nor spite.'
15 B – Para 5: 'Surprisingly, Person 1 generally offers a kind and fair $5/$5 split'
16 A – Para 6: 'Again, the chimpanzee in control gave food to the neighbour only about a quarter of the time'
17 H – Para 7: ' "I don't know why chimps are not other-regarding" '
18 B – Para 2: '… scientists are investigating …'
19 B – Para 3 ' "I get spat on all the time." '
20 B – Para 4: 'Banking, government, and health services all depend on people working for the benefit of complete strangers.'
21 A – Para 5: 'Person 2 generally rejects the offer, docking their own pay as punishment for the other person's selfishness.'
22 C – Para 7: – They share food in the wild but no-one knows why. '"It might be they are unaware of others' needs. It might be they are aware, but unconcerned."'
23 closest genetic relative – Para 2
24 complete strangers – Para 4
25 other-regarding – Para 7
26 mean – Para 8
27 Section A – 7
28 Section B – 5
29 Section C – 2
30 Section D – 4
31 Section E – 1
32 NO – Section B, Para 2: 'But the entire time, you are aware that it's all imaginary.'
33 NO – Section B, Para 3: 'The subject's sense of safety and morality remain entrenched throughout the experience, however. A hypnotist can't get you to do anything you don't want to do.'

34 YES – Section C, Para 3: '…your conscious mind takes a back seat to your subconscious mind.'
35 NOT GIVEN – There is no mention of this anywhere.
36 YES – Section E, Para 3: 'The success of hypnotherapy is undeniable … even if the hypnotic state is nothing more than a figment of the subject's imagination, hypnotic suggestions can still reform their deeply held beliefs.'
37 alert – Section B, Para 1, sentence 5
38 suggestible – Section B, Para 3, sentence 1
39 negative response – Section D, sentence 8
40 inextricably intertwined – Section E, Para 2, sentence 5

Writing p. 96

Task 1 – possible answer

The pie chart gives a breakdown of the sources which Burnland's primary energy came from during the year 2006. All figures are percentages of the total. The country has a heavy reliance on fossil fuels and there is a clear lack of alternative sources.

The most striking feature is Burnland's massive dependence on fossil fuels, which accounted for well over 80% of primary energy supplies. More than 60% came from oil and natural gas combined (36.8% and 23.2% respectively). Coal supplied about a fifth.

The proportion of primary supplies from alternative sources, at under 11%, was very low. More than three-quarters of this was supplied by traditional biomass – in other words, only about 2% of the national total was from modern renewables. Of these the most significant was hydro-electric (1.2%); and about half that amount was supplied by geothermal energy. Modern biomass was insignificant at only 0.2%, while wind and solar energy were the smallest of all, at 0.01% each.

The other primary energy source was nuclear power, accounting for 7.9% of the national total.

(175 words)

Task 2 – model answer

There is a consensus in much of the world that we all have a right to medical care. In my own country, Britain, it is paid for through taxes, making most treatment free at the point of delivery. While I agree with this approach, it will almost certainly have to change.

There is an increasingly wide variety of new and wonderful treatments available. One example is the new generation of drugs which can slow down and even reverse very serious diseases such as cancer. Other treatments, especially in reproductive medicine, are causing a revolution. It is now possible for people to have children much later in life, for instance: famously, an Italian woman in her 60s has recently given birth; and drugs enable men to become fathers much later too.

While wonderful, such treatments change the face of health care radically. At the time the current system was set up, the care available was much more limited and much cheaper. Today we are all living longer – and a single course of treatment with a new wonder drug for one individual can cost tens of thousands of pounds. Despite massive increases in government health spending, there is still a funding crisis which can only get worse.

Put simply, there is not enough money to go round. If we wish to go on providing free health care for all, we will have to limit the types of treatment people can have and this will increasingly mean that new treatments are only available to patients who can pay for them – until the cost falls to an affordable level. This may be the only alternative to abandoning free health care in favour of universal private provision.

(282 words)

Recording scripts

Listening module

Section 1

01

Section 1. You will hear a conversation between a customer and an adviser at a tourist information office. First you have 15 seconds to look at questions 1 to 5.

02

[A = Advisor, C = Customer]

A: Good morning.
C: Hello. Could you help me with some travel information, please?
A: Of course. What do you want to know?
C: Well, I need to get to Harrogate. I'm starting a course there this month and I'm wondering how I can get there.
A: OK, that shouldn't be a problem. What's the name of the place again?
C: Harrogate. Shall I spell that?
A: Yes, please.
C: H-A-double-R-O-G-A-T-E.
A: Thank you. And that's in Yorkshire?
C: That's right.
A: When would you like to travel?
C: Well, next week sometime, I suppose. But the thing I'm wondering about right now is, how to get there, how long it takes and that sort of thing.
A: OK. Well, basically there are two main ways of getting there – by bus or by train. There are direct buses and there are plenty of trains but you have to change.
C: That sounds complicated.
A: Not really. You have to change just once. There are trains via York or Leeds, so you can go via either one.
C: You mean, I can change in York or …?
A: … Or Leeds, yes. It doesn't really make any difference.
C: But the bus is direct, so it's quicker, right?
A: No, I'm afraid not. The bus stops three times en route, so it takes longer.
C: How much difference is there?
A: It varies, depending on what time you travel and how much you pay, but it'll be at least a couple of hours slower by coach.
C: I see.

03

[A = Advisor, C = Customer]

C: So let's say I travel next week. How much will it cost?
A: Which day?
C: Oh, Tuesday – or maybe Thursday. Say Thursday.
A: What time?
C: After lunch. About two, maybe.
A: Going by bus or train?
C: Well, can you give me details for both?
A: OK. And do you want a return ticket?

C: Er … I think just one-way, please, for now.
A: There's a train leaving London at two thirty, getting into Harrogate two hours forty-five minutes later.
C: How about on the bus?
A: Let's see. There's one at two o'clock from Victoria Coach Station. It takes six hours thirty-five minutes.

04

[A = Advisor, C = Customer]

C: How much is the cheapest ticket by train?
A: Have you got a railcard?
C: A what, sorry?
A: A Young Traveller's Railcard. It gives you a 25% discount on rail tickets. You can buy one if you're under 26.
C: No, I haven't.
A: OK. Well, the cheapest rail ticket is sixteen pounds fifty. That's without a railcard.
C: And how much is a railcard?
A: It's twenty pounds.
C: Hmm. It doesn't seem worth it. Does the bus company have a cheaper ticket?
A: Well, the standard fare is £18.75. But the bus company has a student discount card. So that's fifteen pounds if you have a card.
C: And how much is the card?
A: It costs ten pounds. It lasts a year and gets you 20% off all your coach tickets.
C: That sounds pretty good. But then the journey takes so much longer on the bus, doesn't it?
A: Yes, it's six and a half hours on the bus.
C: I think I'll take the train after all. What time does it leave, exactly?
A: At 2.30.
C: That's fine. Can you give me a ticket for that?
A: Of course. I'll need to book you a seat.

05

B C D E G P T V
A H J K
F L M N S X Z
I Y
O
R
Q U W

06

1   0870 225225
2   6.5
3   6.75
4   6½
5   9.20pm
6   9.45am
7   slash
8   at
9   dot

07

1 Two men from Northern Ireland won the Nobel Prize for Peace in <u>1998</u>.
2 Fidel Castro was born <u>August 13th</u>.
3 A return ticket to Paris from London costs <u>40 pounds 14 pence</u>.
4 It takes <u>two and a half hours</u> to fly from London to Rome.
5 It is <u>97 miles</u> from New York to Philadelphia.
6 James Cook landed in Australia in <u>1770.</u>
7 The time difference between London and Shanghai is <u>7 hours</u>.
8 The <u>2004</u> Olympic Games were held in Athens.

08

1 There's a train leaving London <u>Euston</u> – that's E-U-S-T-O-N – at two thirty.
2 There's one at two o'clock from <u>Victoria</u> Coach Station.
3 The postcode is <u>HG2 1JL</u>.
4 The surname is <u>Fauvell</u>, that's F-A-U-V-E-L-L.
5 I've got an offer from <u>Birmingham</u> University.
6 OK, that's – let's see – 124 <u>Warwick</u> Road – that's W-A-R-W-I-C-K Road.
7 The postcode is <u>PB7 9RL</u>.
8 It arrives in <u>Manchester</u> at 16.41.

09

[W = Welfare Officer, S = Student]

W: Welfare Office. Good morning. How can I help you?
S: Um, I think I need to see a dentist.
W: Oh dear, are you in a lot of pain?
S: Well, I chipped my tooth on a bottle last night and it really hurts.
W: Oh, I'm sorry. Whereabouts do you live? So I can give you the name of a dentist near you.
S: In Harbourne.
W: OK. There's a dentist just off the High Street there. That's Mr J. Daunt and Associates.
S: Sorry, could you spell that, please?
W: Yes, that's D-A-U-N-T.
S: Daunt, OK. Do you think I'll be able to see him today?
W: Well, dentists tend to be very busy. You'd have to call them and see. I'll give you the phone number. It's 429 6241.
S: 4-2-9 6-2-4-1. Thanks. And … er do you have the address?
W: The address is 59 Raddlebarn Road. That's R-A-double-D-L-E-B-A-R-N Road.
S: Is there any way to see a dentist quickly?
W: Well, if you explain it's a real emergency, he'll probably see you quite quickly. Why don't you call and see what they say?
S: Yes, I think I will. Thank you very much for your help.

10

[R = Receptionist, S = Student]

R: Mr Daunt's surgery, good morning.
S: Oh, hello. I'm calling to ask if the dentist can see me today. I chipped a front tooth last night and it's really painful.
R: Oh, I see. Um … Well, in that case, let me see if I can fit in an emergency appointment for you. Um … How about 5.30 this afternoon?

S: Oh, yes, thank you.
R: Can I have your name, please?
S: Yes, my name's David Zhang, Z-H-A-N-G.
R: Z-H-A-N-G. Thank you.
S: And can you tell me how much it's going to cost?
R: Well, it depends on how much work Mr Daunt has to do. An emergency appointment is £60.
S: Oh. That *is* expensive. Don't you have a discount for students?
R: Yes, we do. We can give you a 20% discount on the emergency appointment. So it'll be £48. After that we recommend you join our insurance scheme. The normal price is £20 a month. Students pay £15 a month over the year.
S: £15! That's much more than I can afford.
R: We also offer a discount of 15% for students on regular check-ups.
S: Oh, what's the normal price then?
R: A regular check-up usually costs £45. Would you like to come and see Mr Daunt and see what he says?
S: Yes, I think I'd better. My tooth is really hurting.
R: That's fine. See you at 5.30.

Section 2

 11

Good afternoon. My name is Terry Cole and I'd like to welcome you all to this induction session. What I'd like to do this afternoon is to try to give you a brief idea of how the university works and what sort of facilities and opportunities there are here for you. So, if I could start by talking about the way the university is structured. Unlike most universities in this country, we're not a campus university. This means the university is spread throughout the town and there's no one place where you can say it's located. All of you of course belong to a College, and your College is the place where you live. In fact, the university is really an association of all the Colleges. They work together to provide your university education. This means that any kind of questions you may have about accommodation – your room, your meals, your washing – these should be taken up with your College. Your Director of Studies – that's the person responsible for all your courses – is also based in your College and you should go to them for any questions you may have about your work, as they are responsible for your academic life. So the College is the foundation of your life here: your social, as well as your academic, life. But, in addition, the university has Faculties: the History Faculty, Science Faculties, and Engineering Faculty. The Faculties are responsible for the academic organization of the university. Lecturers from all the Colleges work together in the Faculties to plan and teach the programmes of studies. The Faculties also organize all the examinations. Your College has a library, but you may find that your Faculty Library has a larger selection of books available and is more useful for most of your courses. Of course there's also the University Library, which has the most extensive range of books, which you may want to use sometimes. There aren't any sports facilities in the Colleges. For those of you who are interested in sports, there is more information about the Sports Centre on the university website.

12

Now, of course, one of the main things you need to do in these first few days is to find your way around. So let's take a look at some of the local landmarks, some of the most obvious – and most useful – places on the map. So, starting in the town centre – that's towards the bottom of the map – and going out west along Lensman Road, you'll find there are quite a lot of good, inexpensive places to eat along here. But before those, you come to some of the main university buildings – first, the Museum on your right. It's a beautiful, old Victorian building. Then, on the same side of the road, just after the Museum you'll come across a large, glass-built construction surrounded by fountains. That's the Students' Union. You can't miss it. Then, just beyond it, along the footpath, is the Science Faculty. Heading out to the east, along James Street, you'll find the University Library on the left and, just opposite, the Engineering Faculty. But if you're looking for shops, banks and supermarkets you need to be in the town centre. There are lots of narrow streets and it's easy to get lost. If you go north from the town centre, out along John Street, you come first to John's College on the left and, just across the road, one of the main supermarkets. You could almost call it the university supermarket because it's used so much by students – the prices are very competitive. Across the river on the left is the castle. And opposite the castle there's the sports centre. If you go a little further on, across Ripley Road, you'll come to the swimming pool. So, that's a brief tour. We can't show you everything there is in town, and at this stage that would probably be pretty confusing anyway. Are there any questions?

 13

Hi, I'm Jenny Parkside. I'm the President of your local Students' Union here at the University and I'm going to tell you about some of the great things we do in the Union. First of all, the Union is the centre of student social life. As you've seen, we have a brand new Union building in Lensman Road. There are three dining rooms and two bars, open seven days a week, which serve food at very reasonable prices. So, if you don't feel like paying high prices for your meals in town, you can always eat at the Union. During the week we have stand-up comedy shows and live entertainment in the bars, and at weekends there are all-night live bands at the night club. We run a huge range of clubs and activities for everyone including sports clubs: um … rowing, golf, tennis, badminton, you name it. Our members take part in all kinds of fundraising activities for charity and we have countless associations that support activities from film-making to mountain climbing.

Now, I'll tell you a little about the more formal functions of the Union. First and foremost, we represent your interests across the board: social, financial, educational and cultural. As an executive, we have the job of negotiating issues on your behalf that may affect you as a student. It's our job to consult with you and raise your concerns at university committee meetings, including the Senate and Faculty Boards. The Union executive also coordinates with local organizations to promote good relationships between the student and the local population: what we call 'Town and Gown' relations. We take an active part in presenting a positive image of the student body. We also represent your views and support your rights in cooperation with other student unions across the country. In short, we have your welfare and your interests at heart.

Section 3

 14

[S = Steve, A = Angela]

S: Angela, hi. How are you?
A: Good, thanks, Steve. Enjoying this weather. How about you?
S: Well, I'm just starting my final year and I'm getting worried.
A: Ah, exam nerves?
S: Hmm, not yet. But I didn't do very well in my last exams and if I don't do better this year, I'm not going to get the jobs I want. You did well. What's the key to getting a good degree?
A: Well, where do you think you went wrong?
S: Oh, I just don't think I studied properly. I mean, what did you do in your final year?
A: Work!
S: OK, but how did you go about it?
A: I think the most useful thing I did was that I planned everything in detail at the beginning of the year. I looked at the targets I had for the summer and worked backwards from there. I made a list of everything that had to be done before the exams, from September onwards.
S: Sounds depressing!
A: Well, the thing is that then you know exactly what you need to do and you can make a timetable. I worked out what I was going to do during every week of that year.
S: Did you stick to the plan?
A: Pretty much. It really helped, actually, because it made sure I covered everything but it also forced me to be realistic about how much I could do, so I just dropped things when time ran out, because otherwise you could just go on forever!
S: Yeah, that sounds like a good move, and I know organization is one of my weak points. What else?
A: Well, I chose which subjects I was going to do pretty carefully. Don't do *Twentieth Century History*, for example. It's fascinating, but just too big to do in ten weeks. So that's essential. But, on the other hand, you have to get some enjoyment out of it, so it's a good idea to choose at least some subjects you're really interested in.

 15

[S = Steve, A = Angela]

S: I'd be glad of some ideas for my dissertation, especially about reading. There's just so much that's been written on the subject and I can't read it all.
A: Well, you need to know what the main authors think, and you have to read three or four of them in detail. But you certainly don't need to read 25 books from start to finish.
S: No. Time's short. I need to start writing at the beginning of next month, so that gives me three weeks for research.
A: The best starting point on the subject is Bradley's book, I'd say. It covers all the issues and gives you a really good overview.
S: That's a help.
A: You also need to read Peter Holland's book. It has an interesting new way of looking at things and if you look at Johnson that'll give you a solid idea of how people were thinking in the 80s and early 90s, which is essential.
S: Good. I was thinking I'd look at those – and Murry.

A: Murry's interesting but he covers much the same stuff as Johnson in much the same kind of way. I'd read Johnson if I were you. What else? Richards has some really unusual ideas. It's hard to know what to make of them but they can liven up a tired mind. I'd certainly have a look. You could probably get away with reading the last chapter – it's a good summary of his argument.

16

[K = Kimberly, J = Jim]

K: Hi, Jim. How's things?
J: All right. How are you, Kimberly?
K: I'm OK. I'm a bit worried about this presentation we've got to do.
J: Next week, yeah?
K: So what are we going to say?
J: Good question. No idea!
K: Suppose we try to plan it out now, OK? Then we'll have more of an idea of what we need to do.
J: OK, yeah, good move. So, we have to talk about the business we set up as part of our coursework last year.
K: Uh huh. Suppose we just list some ideas about things we could say. That way we'll be able to choose some headings for the presentation.
J: OK. Like what? Where do we start?
K: Oh, we've got to give an overview at the start – what the idea for the business was, how we first got it, why we chose it, that sort of thing.
J: You're right. We've got to show them some of the products too.
K: Yeah, that'd be fun. They'll enjoy passing them around the room and we'll get a few laughs.
J: Right. You know, for me, after we got the basic concept sorted out, the most important thing was working out the money – how we were going to grow the business and sustain sales, all that kind of thing.
K: Don't you think people are going to go to sleep if we start showing them spreadsheets and talking them through the accounts? I think we should go easy on that side of things, give them a couple of figures, no more, and just leave the accounts out …
J: Yeah, a lot of people wouldn't follow them anyway …
K: … but we *must* talk about the marketing side – how we developed the approach to selling that got things up and running.
J: Yeah. Maybe we need to talk about where the start-up cash came from.
K: I think we can leave that out. They can ask if they want to know.
J: You know, it could be useful to roleplay a sales conversation.
K: Yeah, if we have time.
J: And then we could finish up with a question-and-answer session. That ought to take up five or ten minutes!
K: I'm not so sure I like the sound of that! We could end up getting asked something really embarrassing. Are you sure there's going to be time, anyway?
J: OK, OK – questions if time allows. So, do you want to kick off with the overview?

17

K: So … Would you do it all again?
J: What? Set up a business? Definitely, it's the most fun I've had with coursework ever. Changed my mind about university – because it wasn't just studying. It was really practical.

K: Didn't you think one of the best things about it all was the excitement?
J: Yeah, right. I never imagined that running a business could be so exhilarating.
K: And the other part I thought was absolutely fantastic was actually making a profit.
J: Uh huh. I couldn't seriously believe we never ran out of money. In fact, it started flowing in pretty steadily after the first term, didn't it? But I'll tell you what did take me by surprise and that was the hard work. There wasn't a moment's rest, was there?
K: No. It was exhausting. I had no idea running a business was going to be so time-consuming. You couldn't do something like that in your evenings and days off *and* work at a full-time job.
J: No, you couldn't … and in the real world you'd have to control the accounts more carefully. I wish I'd attended more of those first-year company accounts lectures. As it was, I had to learn all that stuff from scratch.
K: Really? You mean you'd forgotten it all, or you just never studied any of it?
J: I just didn't go to many lectures, so I didn't learn much at all.
K: And another difference … with real life you'd have to have a more detailed business plan. I mean, if the bank's going to lend you money to get things off the ground …
J: That's true. The banks need to know you're going to be a fairly small risk before they part with their money … So, what do you think, Kimberly? Shall we go ahead with a real business next year?

Section 4

18

In today's lecture we're going to take a look at a relatively new professional sector called construction site logistics management, which involves the organization and supervision of large-scale building contracts on site. First, we'll see why this new profession has evolved, then we'll have a brief glimpse at what a site logistics management team does and the kind of projects it controls, and finally, I'll outline some of the advantages of this kind of management both for construction companies and individual professionals.

In the past – twenty years ago, say – there was no such thing as construction site logistics management. Construction companies simply competed for projects and, if they were successful, they did the building themselves or formed a consortium to share the work.

These days, as I'm sure you're all aware, managing a large building contract is a much more complex process than it was in the past. Nowadays it involves coordinating a wider range of professionals on a large scale. For instance, an international construction project will use the services of an assortment of legal, financial, commercial and human resource specialists. We should also recognize that, in this day and age, the building industry is more accountable to society than it used to be. For example, on a specific project, a construction company may have to take ecological issues into account and deal sensitively with powerful pressure groups that want to protect our natural surroundings.

So this is the kind of environment in which site logistics management evolved. What exactly do construction site logistics managers do? Well, they're involved in a remarkable range of activities. They may simply supply the equipment needed on the site. Or they might provide the construction workers. Another function could be to manage the whole site – so they might bring in a complete management team. In some cases they'll supply and manage everything on the site including materials, machinery, labour, transport, and security services.

So what kind of project will a construction site logistics management team work on? The kind of project involved can vary enormously. It could be anything from a big civil engineering project to constructing a single building. So, the project may involve digging a tunnel through the Alps, constructing a hydro-electric power station complete with dam or building a new department store.

Now, I'd like to turn to some of the advantages of logistics management. First, let's consider the advantages of this type of management for building contractors. Well, by employing a site logistics management team to control certain aspects of the project, contractors can be free to focus on the activities they are more specialized in. Another benefit is that they can cut their costs by employing experts for specific functions as and when they need them, rather than employing them on a permanent basis.

What are the benefits of this kind of work for the individual professional? For those who enjoy travel and working in an international environment, this kind of work offers an exceptional variety of opportunities. Large-scale construction is, of course, an increasingly international field and, in fact, it's an example of how work in the modern world can flow from one place to another. Today's site logistics manager may spend up to a couple of years working on a major project, hundreds or thousands of miles from home, be it in the north of Scotland, in Siberia or in Romania. Today, for example, there are tremendous opportunities in Central Europe, as the infrastructure of the new accession countries is brought up to date. Poland has had a thriving construction sector for more than ten years now, and the Czech Republic is also developing rapidly.

 19

Good afternoon. Today we continue our series of talks on career opportunities for graduates in commerce and industry.

To begin with we'll be looking at sectors offering openings to graduates from a wide variety of disciplines. Although retailing is thousands of years old, it is paradoxically one of the fastest-moving business sectors, responding quickly to changes in fashion and technology. Looking at retailers today we can see that they combine a number of different approaches to the customer, so that you may find yourself working in a traditional high street store, or for an e-tailer, a retailer who sells on the internet.

Now let's turn to how you get into retail. The first thing to say is that there are some obvious graduate entry routes. For instance, a degree in Business Management could be one and Information Technology another. But more than most fields, retail welcomes non-specialists. If you choose retail, you'll find yourself in competition with bright, ambitious managers who went straight into business from school and could already have anything up to six or seven years' experience, much of it perhaps in management. Most of them will have started at the bottom, as an assistant on the shop floor, and this can be a huge advantage because it teaches you the business from the inside out.

So retail is an exciting business and one that the alert and ambitious can do well in: the rewards can be very high. But it's also a business, as I've already implied, where you need to be fast-moving and flexible yourself. Think about the big high street department stores and how they've changed in recent years. A decade ago they were radically different businesses from today: long-established companies doing very well the same things they'd done for decades, introducing new products here and there but essentially no different from a generation earlier and making, some of them, quite astonishing profits – over a billion pounds a year in one case. And then almost overnight things changed. They faced expert, fast-moving challenges from new, smaller, competitors – the 'verticals' as they became known – such as Gap and Zara. And secondly, the technology changed, almost beyond recognition. Today those same department stores are no longer the high street giants they were. They are multi-channel retailers, selling through the internet, through designer outlets, through small, specialist shops using their own brand name, perhaps through mail order – and of course through their high street stores, which now look like those of the verticals.

 20

Now let's take a few minutes to look at some of the ways in which technology has changed the retail sector in the last decade. A major change is the till system – the cash machines in stores. A generation ago the till was simply a machine for keeping money in and printing receipts. Today it's part of a vast electronic tracking system which can identify individual products – this pair of jeans or that belt – and tell the store's head office when to send more to the store.

One of the most recent technological changes has been RFID – radio frequency identification – the system which allows the store to track every single item of stock through electronic tags attached to the merchandise.

There are various types of tags, which can be passive (that is, they don't have a power source) or active (in which case they have a built-in battery). They all contain information about the products they're attached to and can be read by a number of devices. These devices may be built into the till or they may be the kind you can carry around – a hand-held device. They register the information on the tag electronically and pass it to a computer. This computer may be an ordinary PC or a more powerful computer. The computer, in turn, has an Ethernet connection to a network. In this way it's possible for the store to track stock automatically.

So, what are the rewards of a career in retail and what are some of the possible routes?

Speaking module

Part 1

 21

Interview 1
[E = Examiner, C = Candidate]

E: Can you tell me your name, please?
C: My name is Chung Li Rong.
E: What name shall I use today?
C: Oh, please call me Lee – that's the name I use in English.
E: OK. Thanks, Lee. And where are you from?

C: From Shanghai, in China.
E: And can I see your identification, please?
C: Of course.

 22

Interview 2
[E = Examiner, C = Candidate]

E: I'd like to talk about what you do. Are you a student?
C: Well, I've been studying recently for this test, but no, I work in a care home for elderly people.
E: Do you enjoy that?
C: Er, it can be frustrating at times, but mostly yes, very much. It's a huge privilege to be able to help people who are coming to the end of their lives. Some of them have given a lot to other people in many ways but now they may find some quite simple things quite difficult. It's very rewarding to be able to help them and make their lives easier.
E: Why did you choose that occupation?
C: Actually, I'm a nurse. I've been working in nursing for years and I hope to do that in the UK – but first I need to do IELTS. In the meantime I'm supporting myself by working as a care assistant.

 23

Interview 3
[E = Examiner, C = Candidate]

E: What do you like doing in your free time?
C: I have a very busy job. I don't have free time!
E: What do you **like** doing in your free time?
C: Er … actually, you know, I played football a lot before … er … but now I have no time and … er …
E: What do you like about football?
C: It's good. Er … I like football. Because it has many things … it's exciting.
E: Are there any things you don't like about football?
C: Er … you know …
E: Are there any things you don't like about football?
C: Er … I think everything is good. I like everything about football. It relax me, you know.

 24

Interview 4
[E = Examiner, C = Candidate]

E: Can you tell me your name, please?
C: My name Xiang Chen.
E: What shall I call you?
C: You can call me John.
E: OK. Thanks, John. And where are you from?
C: I'm from Changsha, the capital of Hunan province in China. Hunan is a very old province with an interesting history. Its name means 'Lake South'. But we have the same name, because it sometimes called Xiang for the Xiangjiang River which runs through the province. Xiang has population 63 million and …
E: OK. What do you do …?

 25

Interview 5
[E = Examiner, C = Candidate]

E: What do you like doing in your free time?
C: Well, you know, I really don't have much time these days

because I have a busy job at the hospital and when I'm not working I'm looking after the children at home. So it's really true to say that I have almost no free time. If I had some time for myself, I would read more.
E: What do you enjoy about reading?
C: Oh, I love reading! When I was a child, I used to read all the time. The thing is, you can learn so much from reading – you can understand so much about the world and the people in it and you can learn so much about what's new by reading magazines and newspapers. One of the things I really enjoy is the *New Scientist* because it's always full of interesting things about developments in science and it has some really good, odd, quirky things in it. They did a piece recently on 13 things that just don't fit with our current understanding of the universe, for instance.
E: What kind of books do you enjoy reading?
C: Oh, novels – contemporary novels, especially – but I must admit I have a weakness for detective stories and I do miss those. These days pretty much all the reading I do is for my work – professional journals.
E: Are there any kinds of books you don't like?
C: Absolutely. I loathe science fiction.
E: Why?
C: Well, let's just say my husband reads anything with an alien on the cover but I prefer reading about real things and real people – or at least realistic, if not real!

 26

Interview 6
[E = Examiner, C = Candidate]

E: What do you like doing in your free time?
C: Well, you know, I like to driving. I have a four by four and I like to drive it a lot. Sometimes I drive around the centre of the city and watch people to see who is there and what they looking like and what they are wearing and what they doing, who they are with and like this. There are some special places I like to do this because also it is good that people see you, so also I like to dress well and wear smart clothes so people will see me and know I am a smart person. Sometimes my friends and I we like to drive on the highway. We have a long highway it is mostly very straight and you can drive very very fast here when it is not too busy. In the morning people going to work and in the afternoon people going home and the highway very very busy. But other times it is quiet and you can drive fast, specially at night. This is very good. Also I like to go camping sometimes in my car and …

Part 2

 27

I would like to talk about a machine, a machine I have, it is mine, it is a computer. This computer is very special to me. My parents gave it to me. It is a really good computer, also it looks really cool. It has a slimline tower and I have some really powerful loudspeakers. I kind of wanted a notebook – you say notebook or laptop? – but I need a lot of power sometimes and if you want a lot of power in a notebook that's very, very expensive so I talked about it with my parents, what we could afford, and I decided a PC, like for my desk, would be better because with this I can do many different things. I like to do many, many things with this computer. I like to go online and I spend a lot of my free time online it's good because you can go in chat rooms and you can talk to friends. Maybe some of these friends are really friends, you know, like people you know in your studies or in your university, but also other friends who maybe I have never met in my life because they live in … er different parts of the world, like sometimes I play chess with a guy in Russia. I mean, like I've never been to Russia and maybe I'll never go, but I have a friend there and that's cool. But you can do a lot of other games on the internet, I mean like online gaming and that's really cool, like you can be playing in this … environment with different people at the same time and they can be anywhere you know? Sometimes I like to try out new games too like on CDs and I have some friends, we get a lot of these CDs and we swap them so you can try a lot of good programmes and games without like you know need to buy them all and you see which one you like. Also I like very much to download music and I have an i-pod so I like to use my computer in this way too and it's a bit the same with movies. I like to make video films and I can edit them with my computer.

 28

Candidate 1

I love Lone Pine. It's near Brisbane in Australia, actually just outside Brisbane, I think. I visited some friends who live in Brisbane and they suggested I could go there. I got a bus from the city and it took half an hour. It's a big park or something like that. There are many different kinds of animals. They are interesting animals, too. I saw so many different kinds. There were koalas and kangaroos and I think maybe the other kind – what's that called? – wall … wallabies. Also there were snakes and I have a picture of me holding a snake! I liked the lorikeets best. It made an impression on me because there are so many kinds of animal I had never seen anywhere before.

 29

Candidate 2

Actually, I'd like to talk about my favourite place in England, which is York Minster – that's the Cathedral in the city of York. I never heard this word, Minster, before I went there. I thought maybe it was some special kind of minister but I soon found this was wrong. I know about York Minster because I was studying English near there in Harrogate and they told me in the language academy I must visit the Minster in York. So I took the train, which was just half an hour, and then to reach the Minster from the station is easy, only ten minutes on foot. And I can say this Cathedral is really one of the great buildings of Europe. It's a very special piece of architecture, so beautiful, with such fine lines, so tall. I have seen many wonderful buildings, and many of the great Gothic cathedrals, and this is absolutely my favourite. So I walked around this cathedral and enjoyed the arches, the sculptures and the ceiling especially, until I came to the east end. And here something quite unexpected for me happened. There is a place – just behind the, I can say, the formal part of the cathedral – where you can sit. It's very impressing, astonishing – not so much because of what it looks like but because of how it makes you feel. There is a space between where you can sit and look at the final, east wall, which is only a few metres from you, perhaps three or four – and most of this east wall is in fact windows, wonderful stained glass windows. So I sat down and looked up at the windows and slowly something quite unexpected happened to me. There is a kind of quiet, a hush, which slowly comes into you as you sit there. And soon you can feel the peace of the place, and how people have come here for hundreds of years to sit and be silent and peaceful, thousands and thousands of people, for hundreds and hundreds of years. This is something

truly special. I have found such a feeling only in a few places, but this is one of those places, where just to be there can give you this silence inside.

 30

Candidate 3

I want to talk about my favourite place, it is Whitby, you know, this is where I am living now that I am living in UK, having come here by plane from my country. I came here, have come here, for my job, so I am working now in Whitby. Whitby is in Yorkshire and it is very fine because, you know, there we are having the sea of course and at home we are having the sea also, so this is wonderful for me because it is like a little, I mean, like a glimpse of home. I have lived there now for three months. I will tell you now why … er … it is my favourite place. I like this town because you know it looks very fine, quite romantic, there are many good things you can do and the – er – the harbour is so beautiful. Also the hills next to the harbour, they are so steep. You can climb up many steps to the top, where there is a building, er, you know, church, er, abbey, it is empty, you know the walls are broken and now nobody live there but it looks like you know something from a horror movie or something like that. This is something I never saw before in my life and I am liking this so much, like I feel this is the real England, also because you know the people they are so kind, so very kind, almost I feel like I am in my home in this place and it is exciting because here is beginning a new, er, new part of my life and so now this is my most favourite, so if I would have the same choice again you know I will make the same decision.

 31

Candidate 2
[E = Examiner, C = Candidate]

E: Have you been there again since then?
C: Yes, a number of times. I always make a point to visit this Minster every time I am in the north of England. Last year for example I was on holiday with my wife and children. We have two children, you know, one is eight and the other is nine – both girls – and we decided this year we would go camping because the girls are old enough to manage everything you have to do when you go camping and also it would be a good way for all of us to improve our English! So …
E: I'd like to talk about something else now …

 32

Candidate 3
[E = Examiner, C = Candidate]

E: Have you been there again since then?
C: Yes … thank you.

 33

Candidate 1
[E = Examiner, C = Candidate]

E: Have you been to the animal park again since then?
C: No, I haven't had a chance yet. But I love Australia, especially Queensland, and I'm planning to go back and stay with my friends again. I will definitely go there again when I do.

Part 3

 34

Candidate 1
[E = Examiner, C = Candidate]

E: Do you think it's true that people today generally experience more stress than 50 years ago?
C: Er … more stress?
E: Yes, is life today more stressful than 50 years ago?
C: Ah, stressful. Yes, I think today's lifestyle is very stressful. Everywhere today there is too much stress. Stress for students is very bad. In my country students have to work so hard. Er … First in the place, at school they must study hard and they must study many, many hours after school. They must work very hard for exams and there are too many exams. Then university also very stress. And then you must get job and this too is very hard for many people because it is very competition for the best jobs. If you don't get the best jobs, you don't have chance for earn the best salary and have good life for yourself and your family. So I think this hard for young people and too much stress.

 35

Candidate 2
[E = Examiner, C = Candidate]

E: Do you think it's true that people today generally experience more stress than 50 years ago?
C: That's an interesting question. And quite complex. I think it depends where you live. In my country we have experienced some conflicts, especially in this time you talk about. There is sometimes fighting – not all the time, it comes and it goes – but of course this situation means uncertainty. You do not know what will happen. So it is difficult to plan your life. What studies will you do, where will you live, how will you build your career? These are not questions you can always think about because you don't know if you and your family and your friends will be safe. This is very stressful. So in this way I would have to answer that life is more stressful today – but I have said already this depends on where you live. In many countries today people talk about stress and they mean that they must work hard but their lives are also very comfortable because they have all things they need and they have many luxuries too. Probably the life of their parents and grandparents was not so comfortable.

 36

Candidate 3
[E = Examiner, C = Candidate]

E: How have communications changed in your lifetime?
C: Communications?
E: Yes, the ways that people communicate with each other.
C: I'm sorry, could you explain more, please?
E: People sometimes say there has been a revolution in communications. They mean things like the internet.
C: Ah! Thank you. I think there has been very big change in this area. Maybe the most obvious change now the mobile phone. My uncle he studied in England thirty years ago. In that time he was very lonely because he was far from our family and everything here very strange for him. He told me it was hard for him sometimes to talk on the phone with our family and friends and sometimes he had to wait a long time on the phone to make his call to our

country because in that time it was not possible just to call right away to another country if it was far away. This was very difficult for him because he stayed here a few years – first he studied English language and then he went to university here. For me it is very different – I have my mobile. If I want to talk with my father, my mother, my brothers and sisters, my friends, I can do this and there is no delay, just instant. Also, of course, we send email so it is not difficult and very cheap, even free. Every day I can email my friends and it doesn't matter where we are – sometimes my friends are in different countries. So I think this is very good – big change and much better than before.

Practice test

Section 1

 37

[R = Reader, L = Librarian]

R: Good morning.
L: Morning. Can I help you?
R: Well, I'd like to join the library, please – and there's a specific book I need as well.
L: OK, that's fine. Now, I'll have to put all your details into the system. Just a minute … Ah. Could I have your name, please?
R: It's Mahmoud Alnazri.
L: Is that M-A-H-M-U-D?
R: Er, no, it's O-U-D.
L: Sorry. And could you spell your surname, please?
R: A-L-N-A-Z-R-I.
L: And what's the address?
R: It's 195 Hills Road.
L: 195 Hills Road … and do you know the postcode?
R: I'm sorry, I don't.
L: Never mind. Do you have a phone number?
R: Yeah, it's 07942 116470.
L: Now I'm putting you down for individual student membership. That means your membership is free, but there are some services you'll have to pay for …
R: What kind of services?
L: Oh, if you want to request a book we haven't got on the shelves and we have to order it from storage. Or if you want to borrow CDs or DVDs.
R: I see.
L: Now, did you say there's a book you wanted to see this morning? I can tell you how to find it.
R: Yes, thanks. I've got the details written down here.
L: Let me see … Oh dear … *Listening Skills for Students* …
R: What is it?
L: I'm afraid we'll have to request it from storage – I can input the details here – and you'll have to pay a fee.
R: How much is that?
L: It's a dollar fifty per book.
R: OK. Well, could you order it for me, please?
L: Of course … right. Now you can come back this afternoon and it should be here.
R: What time?
L: Oh, say half past two, to be safe. And you'll need this reference number – do you want to jot this down?
R: OK.
L: It's RBC 09 61 09. Got that? Give it to the librarian when you come back.

R: Right, thanks. So I need to come back here for about two thirty.

L: That's right. It might be here before that, but two thirty should be safe.

R: Is there anywhere round here I could get something to eat while I'm waiting?

L: Of course. There's a canteen here in the library.

R: Good. Which way is that, please?

L: Go along the corridor just here, past the Lecturers' Reading Room and carry on down to the very end. That's the Main Reading Room. Go in and turn right. The canteen's just through the door half way down the room. You'll see the sign.

R: Thanks, that's great. And I need to use a computer as well. Where can I do that?

L: Well, there are PCs all over the building, but the main computer suite is right next to the canteen, in fact. Or there's another door into it from the main entrance, just over there on the left.

R: And the toilets?

L: The toilets are opposite the Lecturers' Reading Room, second on your left as you go down the corridor.

R: Thanks very much.

Section 2

 38

Good morning. What I'd like to do in this first session is to give you some ideas about how you can settle in, both in the city and the university. Every year we support a few hundred students from other countries, and today we want to give you the benefit of their experiences. For example, can you guess what the most common overall worry is for international students during their time here? Studying in English, you might think, or money worries – but in fact the majority say that making friends is their biggest concern. You'll probably find – last year's intake of foreign students certainly did – that your biggest problem in Week 1 isn't making friends, or English, or money, but simply understanding what is going on. It can be a confusing time! By the end of the year, though, for most of last year's international students, academic worries had replaced social and other concerns as the number one issue. I'll come on to make some detailed suggestions in a few minutes, but in the meantime let me just say I think your main priority this week should be to meet people. Also important, of course, is to find out about living here, where things are, where to go at particular times, where the various facilities are and so on. And you need to find out something about the town too. Perhaps the best advice I can give you about that is to get a bike. Cycling is usually the easiest way around the place. It's quicker than walking and cheaper than the bus – and … er probably more reliable too!

There's a huge number of events this week – really more than you can possibly get to – and part of the fun is choosing. But there are certain things that I think you must make sure you get to. These suggestions are based on comments made by students in previous years, by the way. The Language Centre has a seminar on Tuesday to show you the kind of support they can give you with the English language. They offer a great deal more than I could describe at the moment. But one thing I would suggest right now is: they have an excellent computer laboratory at the language centre and it's a good idea to use it as much as possible in your spare time, especially during the first term. The second 'must-see' session is a lecture called Managing Your Money. This has all kinds of helpful

suggestions about your finances; but the main one I'd like to underline now is how important it is for you to open a bank account at once. The lecture, by the way, is provided by Smith's Bank, but you could of course use any of the banks in town – there's not much difference between them. Finally, there are more than fifty university clubs and societies, and joining one or two is an excellent way to meet people and make friends.

They have informal meetings going on all week – you can see the details on the handout. What I'd like to say about these is, choose something that interests you and go along. Finally, we have a very informative student newsletter. You should all have a copy in your orientation pack. It's a good idea to check it for details of club events.

Section 3

 39

[R = Richard, P = Dr Poole]

R: Hello, Dr Poole. I'm glad you're in. Have you got a few minutes, please?

P: Sure, Richard. Come on in. What can I do for you?

R: Well, I'm really confused at the moment and I was wondering if we could talk about my Chinese language.

P: What, the lectures or the reading or what?

R: No, I feel OK with that side of things. What's bothering me is really how to study the language itself.

P: Ah, the private study aspect.

R: That's right. You see, I've studied Spanish and French and was able to use them quite a lot on holiday and I met a lot of people I could practise with. But this is completely different – I have no idea where to start and no one I can practise with. I don't even know if I've got the right books.

P: Well, the books on the reading list are fine. You can keep working with those. Let's work out a study plan and get your priorities clear.

R: And my pronunciation is just terrible and I don't know how to improve it.

P: Hmm. Remember, we're dealing with a language that's really different from English, French or Spanish so you probably need to take a different focus. I see pronunciation less as something to do a lot of intensive work on and more as something that'll develop with practice and experience. Don't lose sleep over it at this stage.

R: I sometimes think I should just drop the course and go to China. Then maybe I could come back and study more. Would I be able to start the course again next year?

P: Well, you might, although I can't guarantee that. But I think you'll get much more benefit from a stay in China next year. I think you should concentrate on learning more of the basics first.

R: You mean grammar?

P: Yes. I think your priority for now should be to get really familiar with the grammar. Focus your private study on the language structures at the moment. The key is the written language. So you should dedicate as much time as you can to studying the way the language is written. Get plenty of practice, and then next semester you can start building up your vocabulary more.

R: So you don't think I should drop out of the course?

P: Not at all. I think the problems you're having are pretty normal ones, especially for someone who's not really used to learning a language in its written form. I think what you need to do most is improve your motivation. Look for opportunities to get into the language. You want to go to China so make that a target, a reason for improving.

R: There's a scholarship competition for students who want to visit China.

P: So make an application. And think about what there is here, in the local environment, that you can use. There are plenty of Chinese students around. You can probably arrange some exchange classes with one of them – you speak English with them, they help you with writing basic Chinese sentences. Have you joined the China Society?

R: Yes, but I haven't been to any meetings yet.

P: Well, use them. It's a chance to hear people speaking – and to see Chinese films.

R: I'll do that.

P: At this stage you won't understand everything and you can say very little, but you're laying foundations. Chinese is really different so work on developing your mental flexibility. Read simple books. Read popular magazines. Start getting familiar with the way sentences are organized.

R: What about speaking?

P: Well, that will really come later, when you know more. But what you can do now is lots of listening. It'll pay off later. Watch TV. Go to those meetings. You can just sit and listen and join in when you're ready – maybe next year! Don't worry if you can't say anything – you won't be the only one!

Section 4

 40

In today's lecture we take a look at the background to the recent interest in spas – the natural water springs – and the towns built on those springs, where people go to bathe and drink 'the waters'.

We tend to assume that treatment with water – often in luxurious surroundings – is a modern phenomenon. Nothing could be further from the truth. The idea of immersing yourself in water for the sake of better health – whether of mind, body or spirit – is very old, perhaps as old as humanity. In Finland, hot springs were exploited three thousand years ago for saunas. The Japanese used hot springs too. It's reported that the first one opened at Izumo in 737 B.C. It's interesting to note that leisure complexes developed here, although some hundreds of years afterwards. We know from writers including Homer that the ancient Greeks had a number of forms of social bathing as early as 500 B.C., as did the Babylonians and later the Romans. The bath house is of course often cited as one of the Roman Empire's lasting contributions to civilization in the countries they ruled, although they may not have been the first to use natural waters in this way. The first large-scale public baths were constructed in 25 B.C. We like to think that leisure centres are a modern idea. In fact, the Romans certainly had the same concept two thousand years ago and the bath houses evolved into complexes which included restaurants, for example, as well as other forms of entertainment – a concept which, as we know, the Japanese had created previously.

The early history of spas in Britain is not entirely clear. Legend has it that King Lear's father, Blalud, was cured of leprosy by the hot mud at Bath in 863 B.C. and that he founded the town of Bath as a result. Certainly the Romans developed an important spa centre there. This is hardly surprising, given that it is the only place in Britain where springs provide a continuous supply of hot water at about 50 degrees Celsius. Public baths seem to have fallen into disuse after the Romans left, but came into favour again during the eighteenth century when, right across Europe, they were considered the height of fashion, with visitors flocking to centres such as Baden Baden in Germany, Evian-les-Bains in France, Saint Moritz in Switzerland and of course Bath, Buxton and Harrogate in Britain, often on the advice of their doctors.

Inherent in all this is the assumption that bathing is good for the health and that the waters may have medicinal value – as in the story about Blalud. Today there is a general feeling that spa treatments are calming for the mind and body. However, there is less consensus about the medicinal value of spa waters. 250 years ago doctors recommended 'taking the waters' for many medicinal purposes. It was regarded as a tonic, to improve the patient's general wellbeing. Many people today would agree that bathing often has such effects.

Spa treatment centres and their proponents claim much more. Bathing in spa waters with a high sulphur content, they say, helps with skin conditions, and very highly carbonated salt waters such as those at Baden Baden and Harrogate have long been thought to help with rheumatism and other conditions. That said, the bathing water used at many spa treatment centres is not in fact spa water, but simply water from the town's mains water supply.

Similar claims are made for drinking spa waters. Some waters, because of their chemical composition, are claimed to clean and improve the general condition of the skin and most are said to have a beneficial effect on the digestion – more so than ordinary water. If we accept that this may once have been true before the development of modern medicine – before doctors had other means of removing parasites from the body, for example – then what effects do today's much higher pollution levels have on ground water?

Finally, there is a third field to consider – bottled water. Many people on earth have no clean water for drinking, washing or cooking. Yet, worldwide, bottled water is a multi-billion-dollar industry. The cost of bottled water in developed countries may be as much as 10,000 times the cost of water from the tap. But is bottled water any healthier than the tap water which costs so much less?

As you can see, there are many questions to be answered and we have only begun to look at the political aspects of water, a resource which will become more and more important, and less and less easy to find – in fact one of the world's biggest political issues – as the century goes on. And this is where we will pick up in our next lecture – looking at water as a geopolitical resource.